The Writings

of

Saint Francis of Assisi

NEWLY TRANSLATED INTO ENGLISH

WITH AN INTRODUCTION AND NOTES

BY

FATHER PASCHAL ROBINSON

of the Order of Friars Minor

PHILADELPHIA

The Dolphin Press

MCMVI

Reprinted by Affinity Imprints,
2022

Imprimi permittitur

Paterson die 26 Novembris, 1905

FR. EDUARDUS BLECKE, O.F.M.

Provinciae SS. Nominis Jesu Minister Provincialis

Imprimatur

✝ PATRITIUS JOANNES

Archiep. Philadelphien.

Die 8 Decembris, 1905

TO THE

MOST REVEREND

Father Denis Schuler

THE ONE HUNDRED AND FIFTH SUCCESSOR OF

SAINT FRANCIS AS MINISTER GENERAL

OF THE FRIARS MINOR

CONTENTS.

viii   *CONTENTS.*

INTRODUCTION.

I.

HE writings of St. Francis may, as is obvious, be considered from more than one point of view. Premising this, we are afforded a clue to the difficulty which has led students of Franciscan sources to divide themselves into two camps as to the objective value of these writings. Indeed, one writer[1] goes so far as to compare the attitude of modern scholars toward them to that of the "Spiritual" and Conventual Friars respectively in the first century of Franciscan history. For while one party, led by M. Paul Sabatier,[2] attaches what some regard as almost undue weight to the writings of St. Francis as a source of our knowledge of him, the other party, following Mgr. Faloci Pulignani,[3] displays, we are told, a tendency to belittle their importance. The truth is, as Professor Müller long ago pointed out,[4] that these writings afford

[1] Prof. A. G. Little. See *English Historical Review*, Oct., 1902, p. 652.

[2] M. Sabatier's views on this point are summarized in his *Vie de S. François*, Paris, 1904. See *Études des Sources*, p. xxxvi.

[3] Mgr. Faloci's opinion may be found in his *Miscellanea Francescana*, Foligno, t. VII, p. 115 seq.

[4] *Die Anfänge des Minoritenordens*, Freiburg, 1885, p. 3.

us little if any information as to the life of their
author, a fact which may perhaps account for
their comparative neglect by so many of the
Saint's biographers, but it is not less true that
they bear the stamp of his personality and
reflect his spirit even more faithfully than the
Legends written down on the very morrow of
his death by those who had known him the best
of all.[1] For this reason they are well worth all
the serious study that scholars outside the Franciscan Order are now beginning to give to them.

To say that the writings of St. Francis reflect
his personality and his spirit is but another way
of saying that they are at once formidably mystic and exquisitely human ; that they combine
great elevation of thought with much pictur-
esqueness of expression.   This twofold element,
which found its development later on in the
prose of mystics like St. Bonaventure and in the
verse of poets like Jacopone da Todi, and which
has ever been a marked characteristic of Franciscan ascetic literature, leads back to the writings of the Founder as to the humble upper
waters of a mighty stream.   St. Francis had the
soul of an ascetic and the heart of a poet. His
unbounded faith had an almost lyric sweetness about it his deep sense of the spiritual is
often clothed with the character of romance.
This intimate union of the supernatural and the
natural is nowhere more strikingly manifested
than in the writings of St. Francis, which, after

[1] See *Opuscula*.   Ed. Quaracchi, p. vi.

the vicissitudes of well nigh seven hundred winters, are still fragrant with the fragrance of the Seraphic springtide.

Important as the doctrinal aspect of St. Francis' writings must of necessity be to all who would understand his life—since "the springs of action are to be found in belief, and conduct ultimately rests upon conviction"—it is foreign to the object of the present volume. I am here concerned with the literary and historical aspect of these writings. Suffice it to say that St. Francis' doctrine,[1] which received, so to speak, the Divine *Imprimatur* upon the heights of La Verna two years before his death,[2] is nothing more or less than a paraphrase of the Sermon on the Mount. Nowhere can there be found a simpler literalness in the following of the "poverty, humility, and holy Gospel of the Lord Jesus" than in the writings of St. Francis, and any attempt to read into them the peculiar doctrines of the Abbot Joachim of Flora, the Humiliati, the Poor Men

[1] See on this subject the long study of Cardinal Gabriel de Treio, given by Wadding in the *Opuscula.* The full title is: "Gabriel, divina miseratione S. R. E. Tituli S. Pancratii presbyter cardinalis de Treio, in epistola missa ad R. admodum P. Lucam Wadingum." It is given in substance by Fr. Apollinaris, O. F. M., in his *Doctrine Spirituelle de S. François* (Paris, 1878). See also the *Bibliotheca Veterum Patrum* (Cologne, 1618), which ranks St. Francis among the Fathers.

[2] ". . . nel crudo sasso, intra Tevere ed Arno,
Da Cristo prese l'ultimo sigillo,
Che le sue membra due anni portarno."

Paradiso, XI—114.

of Lyons, or any of their nameless followers, is as unjust as it is unjustifiable. Needless to add that St. Francis' writings contain no new message. Indeed, the frequency with which certain very old and familiar aspects of the eternal truths are insisted upon by St. Francis in season and out of season, is not unlikely to weary the average reader who does not pause to look between the lines. This tendency to repeat himself, which is habitual with St. Francis, does not necessarily bespeak any dearth of ideas. On the contrary. His simple, childlike nature fastened upon three or four leading thoughts "taken from the words of the Lord," which seemed to him all-sufficing, and these he works into his writings over and over, tempering them to the needs of the different classes he addresses as he understood them. If then we recall the circumstances under which St. Francis wrote and the condition of those for whom his writings were intended in the first instance, far from being bored, we may gain something from each new repetition.

Because St. Francis loved Jesus and His Eucharistic Passion, ardently, enthusiastically, almost desperately—to borrow Bossuet's adjectives—his sympathy extended to every creature that suffered or rejoiced. His writings are eloquent witnesses to this far-reaching, all-embracing solicitude. They may be said to run over the whole gamut. Witness the soft note touched in the letter to Brother Leo and the deep masculine tone in which the Testament is pitched. On the whole, however, his writings fall naturally under three heads:[1] those, like the Rules, which represent St. Francis as legislator; those, like the Letter to a Minister, which show us St. Francis as a spiritual father; and those, like the Praises and Salutations, in which we see St. Francis as his earliest biographer saw him—"not so much a man praying as prayer itself."[2]

It was Matthew Arnold, I believe, who first held St. Francis up to English readers as a literary type[3]—a type withal as distinct and formal as the author of the *Divine Comedy*. But however true a poet—and without St. Francis no Dante—it is certain that the *Poverello* was in no sense a man of letters. He was too little acquainted with the laws of composition to advance very far in that direction. His early years had been a bad preparation for study, and he ever remained a comparative stranger to the ecclesiastical and classical learning of his time, though probably his culture was larger than we might be led to conclude from his repeated professions of ignorance and the disparaging remarks of some of his early biographers. Through his mother he seems to have got some acquaintance

---

[1] See Boehmer, *Analekten*, p. xlv.

[2] " Non tam orans quam oratio factus." 2 Cel. 3, 51.

[3] See his chapter on " Pagan and Mediæval Religious Sentiment " in the *Essays on Criticism*. Third edition, Macmillan, 1875, pp. 243–248.

with French;[1] he received elementary instruction in reading and writing from the priests at
San Giorgio, who also taught him enough Latin
to enable him to write it in later years after a
fashion,[2] and to understand the ritual of the
Church and its hymns, which he was wont to
sing by the wayside. But in considering St.
Francis' literary formation, we must reckon
largely with the education he picked up in
the school of the Troubadours, who at the
close of the twelfth century were making for
refinement in Italy.[3] The imagery of the *chan-
sons de gestes* seems to have exercised an abiding
influence upon St. Francis' life and writings, as
is evident from his own tale of the Lady Poverty, which later inspired the pen of Dante and
the brush of Giotto. Witness, too, his frequent
allusions to the Knights of the Round Table ;
his desire that his Friars should become "the
Lord's Jongleurs," and his habit of courtesy
extended even to Sister Death.[4] On the other
hand St. Francis was nothing if not original.
His writings abound not only in allegory and
personification, but also in quaint concepts and

[1] See *Leg. III Soc.*, 10.
[2] Eccleston speaks of his "false Latin." See below, p. 132.
[3] Some of the greatest troubadours of Provence were then
sojourning in Italy. On their journeys and influence there
see Fauriel, *Histoire de la poésie Provençale*, t. II, and three
articles by the same author in the "Bibliothèque de l'École des
Chartes," t. III and IV. Fragments of their poems are given
by Monaci : *Testi antichi provenzali* (Rome, 1889).
[4] See Görres : *Der hl. Franciscus von Assisi, ein Troubadour* (Ratisbon, 1879).

naïve deductions. His final argument is often a text of Holy Scripture, which he uses with a familiarity and freedom altogether remarkable. Indeed there are parts of his writings in which the interweaving of Scriptural phrases is so intricate as almost to defy any attempt to indicate them by references, the more so since the Bibli cal language adopted by St. Francis is not always taken from the Bible, but often from the Liturgy, Missal, and Breviary.[1] For the rest, as Celano puts it, "he left empty ornaments and roundabout methods of speech and everything belonging to pomp and to display to those who are ready to perish; for his part he cared not for the bark, but for the pith; not for the shell, but for the nut; not for the multiple, but for the one only sovereign good."[2]

If we may judge from the two solitary autographic fragments of his that have come down to us,[3] St. Francis was not by any means a skilful penman. Be this as it may, St. Bonaventure clearly implies that he had a secretary,[4] to whom

[1] I have rendered all Scripture phrases by the corresponding Douay Version; not, indeed, that I wish to raise any vexatious question as to the relative merits of the Douay and the English Authorized Version from a literary point of view, but because, as every student of Franciscan literature must be aware, the Biblical passages in the early documents are quoted from the Vulgate, and the English Authorized Version is not and does not profess to be a translation of the Vulgate. See *Franciscan Annals*, January, 1905, p. 8.

[2] 1 Cel. 1. [3] See below, p. 130.

[4] M. Sabatier (*Vie de S. François*, p. 5) suggests that Brother Leo may have acted in this capacity, and invokes the authority of Bernard of Besse to prove it.

he dictated notes, and affirms with Celano that the Saint signed such documents as called for his signature with the "sign *thau*," or capital *T*.[1] Whether or not St. Francis' practice of signing his name thus has any connection with Brother Pacifico's vision of the large *T*,[2] is a matter of conjecture and of small import. What is certain is that St. Francis wrote little. The most characteristic of his extant writings are very short, extremely simple in style, and without any trace of pedantry. If some of the longer pieces seem to show the touch of a more skilful hand than that of St. Francis, *idiota et simplex*, we need not on this account feel any misgivings as to their authenticity. Whatever assistance he may have received in pruning and embellishing certain of his later compositions from Cæsar of Spires or another, no one who examines these writings carefully can doubt but that they are the work of the great Saint himself.

From a literary standpoint perhaps the most carefully composed bit of St. Francis' writing that has come down to us is the realistic picture of the miser's death in the letter "To all the Faithful." More interesting, however, to the student is the "Canticle of the Sun," not only as an example of the simple, spontaneous Umbrian dialect rhyme which St. Francis taught his poet followers to substitute for the artificial versifica-

---

[1] For the testimony of St. Bonaventure and Celano see below, p. 147.

[2] See Tract. de Miraculis., *Anal. Bol.*, t. xviii, p. 115.

tion of courtly Latin and Provençal poets, but also because of the light it throws on St. Francis' literary method,—if method it may be called. His piecemeal fashion of composing as the spirit moved him, is also manifest in a very different work, the First Rule, as is evident from the modification and additions this strange piece of legislation suffered during the fourteen years it was in force.[1] St. Francis' practice of returning to his old writings, retouching and remoulding them, working them over and inserting parts of them in his new ones, goes far toward explaining difficulties which would otherwise arise from the resemblance between his different compositions.

For the rest, even though St. Francis' literary culture was incomplete, his constant contemplation of the " things that are above " and the perfect purity of his life whetted alike his understanding of supernatural truth and of the human heart, and so it comes to pass that his simple words, written down in the far-off thirteenth century and with a fashion of speech different from ours, yet work wonders to this day, while the tomes of many a learned doctor " leave all things as they were before."

It remains to say a few words concerning the history of St. Francis' writings before coming to the writings themselves.

---

[1] See below, p. 27.

II.

The history of the writings of St. Francis, from the time of their composition in the far-off thirteenth century down to our own day, opens up a most interesting field for speculation. Who, it may be asked, first gathered these writ‧ings together? In answer to this question nothing definite can be said, for the early Legends and Chronicles of the Order are silent on the subject, and we must rest content to begin our inquiry with the oldest MS. collections containing the writings of St. Francis. Many such collections exist in mediæval codices, but any attempt to classify these MSS. is, in the present state of our documentation, beset by peculiar difficulties. Not the least of these difficulties arises from the fact that even as in the Legends or Lives of St. Francis we can distinguish a double current;[1] so, too, in the early MS. collections two distinct families or categories are found representing or rather illustrating the twofold tradition and observance which date from the very beginnings of Franciscan history.[2]

The first place among these collections belongs to the MS. numbered 338, formerly in

[1] See Lemmens : De duobus generibus vitarum S. P. Francisci in *Doct. Ant. Franc.*, P. II, p. 9; and de Kerval : Les Sources de l'histoire de S. François in *Bullettino Critico*, fasc. 1, p. 3.

[2] See Sabatier : *Opuscules*, fasc. **x**, p. 133; also Boehmer : *Analekten*, p. vi.

the Sacro Convento, but now in the municipal
library at Assisi. Critics who have studied this
early codex are not in accord as to its age.[1] But
it dates at least from the beginning of the fourteenth century. It includes eleven of the nine-
teen works here translated. They are contained
in three parchment books in the following order :
fol. 12–16, The Second Rule of the Friars Minor ;[2]
fol. 16–18, The Testament ;[3] fol. 18–23, Admonitions ;[4] fol. 23–28, The Letter to All the
Faithful ;[5] fol. 28–31, The Letter to the General
Chapter ;[6] fol. 31–32, Instruction to Clerics on
the Holy Eucharist ;[7] fol. 32, Salutation of the
Virtues ;[8] fol. 33, The Canticle of the Sun ;[9]
fol. 34, Paraphrase of the Lord's Prayer ;[10]
fol. 34–43, The Office of the Passion ;[11] and
fol. 43, The Regulation for Hermitages.[12]

The same collection either wholly or in part
is given in the well-known fourteenth century
compilation of *materia seraphica* known as *Fac
secundum exemplar* from the opening words of
its prologue, and which may be found in the

---

[1] See Ehrle, S.J. : Die historischen Handschriften des Klos-
ters San Francesco in Assisi in *Archiv für Litteratur*, etc.,
t.I, p. 484 ; Mgr. Faloci Pulignani in the *Miscell. Francescana*,
t. VI, p. 46 ; M. Sabatier : *Vie de S. François*, I, p. 370 ; and Professor Alessandri : *Inventario dei manoscritti della biblioteca
del conv. de S. Francesco di Assisi*, p. 57.

[2] See page 64.   [3] See page 81.
[4] See page 5.   [5] See page 98.
[6] See page 111.   [7] See page 23.
[8] See page 20.   [9] See page 152.
[10] See page 139.   [11] See page 155.
[12] See page 89.

Vatican MS. 4354, the Berlin MS. 196, the Lemberg MS. 131,[1] and the Liegnitz MS. 12.[2] The Mazarin MSS. 989 and 1743,[3] as well as the Düsseldorf MS. 132,[4] may also be said to belong to this family of codices which present the writings of St. Francis in practically the same number and order as Mariano of Florence adopts in his *Chronicle,* composed about 1500.[5]

We now come to the second collection of St. Francis' writings, which is often found along with the traditional *Legenda Trium Sociorum,* and the *Speculum Perfectionis.* It is represented by the celebrated Florentine codex at Ognissanti,[6] the codex ½₂₅ at St. Isidore's, Rome,[7] the Vatican MS. 7650,[8] and the codex of the Capu-

[1] See *Speculum Perfectionis* (ed. Sabatier), p. clxxvi, for description of these three MSS.

[2] See Sabatier: Le Manuscrit de Liegnitz, in *Opuscules,* t. I, p. 33. This codex adds the Salutation of the Blessed Virgin and the letter to Brother Leo.

[3] On these MSS. see *Spec. Perf.* (ed. Sabatier), p. clxiv.

[4] This MS. adds the example: *Fuit quidam miles,* etc. See *Actus B. Francisci* (ed. Sabatier), cap. 66.

[5] The *Chronicle* of Mariano, so often quoted by Wadding, is now lost. It comprised five large volumes in folio. In the first of these he gives the catalogue of St. Francis' writings above referred to, and which is reproduced in the Quaracchi edition after Wadding. I have not deemed it necessary to translate it here. On Mariano and his works, see Sabatier: Bartholi, p. 137.

[6] On this MS. see Minocchi: "La Legenda trium Sociorum," p. 13; also his "Nuovi Studii" in the *Archiv. Storico Ital.,* t. XXIV, p. 266; see also Sabatier: Bartholi, p. cxxxv.

[7] On this MS. see Lemmens: *Doct. Ant. Franc.,* P. III, p. 52.

[8] On this MS. see Sabatier: Bartholi, p. cxlvi.

chin convent at Foligno,[1] all of which contain St. Francis' works in almost the same order as that given by Bartholomew of Pisa, in his *Liber Conformitatum.*[2]

This second collection of the writings of St. Francis differs from the first one in several details. In the first place it omits the Instruction to Clerics on the Holy Eucharist and adds the letter To a Certain Minister.[3] Again, the Assisi and Liegnitz MSS., which are typical examples of the first collection, place the prayer, "O Almighty Eternal God," etc.,[4] at the end of the letter to the General Chapter, whereas in the Ognissanti MS. and others of the same family this prayer is found elsewhere. So, too, in the Assisi and Liegnitz MSS. the Salutation of the Virtues is inscribed "Salutation of the Virtues which adorned the Soul of the Blessed Virgin Mary and which ought to adorn the holy soul," while in the Ognissanti and kindred MSS. the title of this piece reads: "Salutation of the Virtues and of their efficacy in confounding Vices." These examples suffice to indicate that this twofold family of MSS. includes also a two-

[1] On this MS. see Faloci: *Misc. Frances.*, t. VII, p. 45; and Sabatier: *Opuscules*, t. I, p. 359. It may be noted that the Foligno MS. conforms more to that of St. Isidore's and the Vatican MS. rather to that of Ognissanti.

[2] My references to the *Conformities* are to the Milan edition of 1510. The edition published in 1590, especially in the historical part, is mutilated and corrupted at almost every page, as I can personally attest after a comparison of it with several old MS. versions.

[3] See below, p. 121.　　　　[4] See below, p. 118.

fold reading, as becomes more evident from the variants noted elsewhere in the course of this work. Meanwhile, let us pass on from the MS. collections of St. Francis' writings to the

PRINTED EDITIONS.

Two diverse compilations, each containing part of the *Opuscula*, were published at the beginning of the sixteenth century. The first of these, known as the *Speculum Vitae B. Francisci et Sociorum ejus*,[1] and quarried largely from the *Actus Beati Francisci*, contains (fol. 126-127) among various legends and other narrations some of St. Francis' prayers, and (fol. 189) also the First Rule. The second compilation, which is of a much more polemic character,[2] and which contains a larger number of the *Opuscula*, appeared successively with some variations in form at Rouen in 1509 as the *Speculum Minorum*,[3] at Salamanca in 1511 as the *Monumenta Ordinis Minorum*,[4] and at Paris in 1512 as the *Firma-*

[1] It was printed at Venice "expensis domini Jordani de Dinslaken per Simonem de Luere" in 1504, and at Metz "per Jasparem Hochffeder" in 1509. Both these editions are identical. It was republished by Spoelberch at Antwerp in 1620.

[2] It is largely a collection of declarations and expositions of the Rule, and of statutes, decrees, and privileges concerning the Order.

[3] The *Speculum* Morin, as it is called from the printer, Martin Morin, is now very rare. In a copy at the National Library, at Paris, it is ascribed to Fr. John Argomanez, a Spanish provincial. See *Études Franc.*, t. XIII, p. 317.

[4] Also at Barcelona, in 1523. See Sbaralea: *Supplementum*, p. 51.

menta trium Ordinum B. Francisci.[1] The seventeenth century saw the appearance of

WADDING'S EDITION.

The honor of making the first serious attempt
to collect all the writings of St. Francis belongs
to the renowned Annalist of the Order, Father
Luke Wadding.[2] His celebrated edition of the
Opuscula[3] is distributed in three parts: Part I
contains the Letters, Prayers, and the Testament; Part II, the Rules; and Part III, the
Monastic Conferences, the Office of the Passion
and Canticles, followed by Apophthegms, Colloquies, Prophecies, Parables, Examples, Benedictions, etc.

Wadding's edition of the *Opuscula* differs
mainly from all preceding collections in this,
that whereas the latter contained only those
pieces which as regards both matter and form
were the handiwork of St. Francis, Wadding felt
justified in including among St. Francis' writings
many *dicta* of the Saint found in the early
Legends. For example, St. Bonaventure[4] relates of St. Francis "Non enim securum *esse
putabat* earum formarum introrsus haurire im-

---

[1] On the edition published at Venice, in 1513, see Sbaralea:
Supplem., p. 196.

[2] See *The Life of Father Luke Wadding*, by Fr. Joseph
O'Shea, O.F.M.

[3] See Wadding: *B. P. Francisci Assisiatis Opuscula*, Antwerp, 1623. See also his *Scriptores Ordinis Minorum*, p. 112;
and Sbaralea: *Supplem.*, p. 244.

[4] *Leg. Maj.*, V, 5.

agines." Wadding, in his sixth Conference, by changing *putabat* into *puto*, gives this passage as the *ipsissima verba* of St. Francis. Again, in the seventeenth Conference, he entirely changes the form of what St. Bonaventure elsewhere [1] relates of St. Francis when he substitutes " Officium praedicationis Patri misericordiarum omni sacrificio *est* acceptius " for " Istius Miserationis officium Patri misericordiarum omni sacrificio *firmabat* acceptius."

Thus it comes to pass that in Wadding's edition, side by side with the undisputed writings of St. Francis, we find doubtful, even spurious, extracts from different sources attributed to the Seraphic Father. It must ever remain a matter of regret that Wadding, instead of following the oldest MSS. that he had at hand, was content to transcribe the incomplete and often interpolated parts of them he found in second-hand compilations, like that of Mark of Lisbon. His work from our standpoint is vitiated by imperfect research and unreliable criticism. But if Wadding was more profuse than prudent in his attribution of Franciscan fragments to the Founder, it must be remembered that he wrote at a time when even the highest minds troubled themselves little enough about literary exactness. For what we now glorify as "scientific criticism" had not yet become the fashion. The faults therefore of Wadding's edition of the *Opuscula* are largely the faults of

[1] *Leg. Maj.*, VIII, 1.

his time; and considering the difficulties to be overcome, the result of his labors was very creditable. And if he had never undertaken the task of collecting St. Francis' writings, any attempt of ours to that end would be surely more ᐧarduous, and perhaps not so fruitful.

Several editions of St. Francis' writings have appeared since Wadding's day, notably those published by de la Haye,[1] Von der Burg,[2] and Horoy.[3] But these editions are very imperfect. Their authors, in spite of the advance made in historical criticism since Wadding's day, have merely reproduced and rejuvenated the edition of the great annalist. The same is true of the various translations of the *Opuscula*, —they are simply Wadding in Italian,[4] English,[5] French,[6] German,[7] or Spanish,[8] as the case may be.

On the other hand, M. Sabatier's strictures on the "numerous ecclesiastics" who have edited

[1] *Opera Omnia S. Francisci*, Paris, 1641.

[2] *Opera B. P. Francisci*, Cologne, 1849.

[3] *Sti Francisci Assisiensis Opera Omnia*, Paris. 1880 (vol. VI of Bibliotheca Patristica.)

[4] *Oposculi di S. Francesco*, by Fr. Bernardo da Fivizzano, O.M.Cap., Florence, 1880. The Latin text is also given in this edition.

[5] *Works of St. Francis.* Translated by a Religious of the Order. London, 1890.

[6] *Œuvres de S. François.* Trans. of Berthaumier. Paris, 1864.

[7] *Leben, Regel, und Werke des h. Franziskus von Assisi.* By Hereneus Haid. Ratisbon, 1856.

[8] *Obras Completas del B. P. S. Francisco de Asis segun la coleccion del P. Wadingo.* Ternel, 1902.

the writings of St. Francis, for not reprinting
Wadding's comments on them, are a trifle wide
of the mark, seeing that their editions were prepared mainly for a class of readers whose point
of view is practical and devotional, rather than
theoretical and speculative, who read the writings of the saints not merely as historical or
literary documents, but as words of spirit and of
life. For such a clientele critical notes would
be caviare indeed.

The remarkable upgrowth of interest in the
sources of early Franciscan history that has
characterized the literature of the past decade
accentuated the need of a more perfect edition
of St. Francis' writings. The matter was soon
taken in hand by the Friars Minor at Quaracchi
—already famous in the literary history of the
Order—and in 1904 they issued the

FIRST CRITICAL EDITION

of the *Opuscula.* [1] Without overlooking the
internal character of each document, the
Quaracchi editors based their edition upon the
early MS. tradition, weighing by this standard
all the various writings contained in the stereo-
typed editions of St. Francis' works, with the
result that many a familiar page that had come
down to us on the good faith of Wadding was

[1] "*Opuscula Sancti Patris Francisci Assisiensis* sec.
Codices MSS. emendata et denuo edita a PP. Collegii S. Bonaventurae. Ad Claras Aquas (Quaracchi), 1904."

found wanting. Thus the seventeen letters commonly ascribed to St. Francis have been reduced to six, the Rules of the Second and Third Orders have been eliminated, only one of the twenty-eight monastic conferences, and one of the seven blessings, are left; most of the prayers have gone, and all the colloquies, prophecies, parables, etc., have likewise disappeared. Most likely the doubtful and supposititious works thus excluded often embody the doctrine and ideas of St. Francis; to a greater or lesser extent some of them may even be his in substance, but as there is no good reason to believe they are his own composition they are not entitled to a place among his writings.

The authentic works of St. Francis left to us then, according to the Quaracchi edition, are the Admonitions, Salutation of the Virtues, Instruction on the Blessed Sacrament, the First and Second Rules of the Friars Minor, the Testament and Regulation for Hermitages, some fragments from the Rule of the Clares, Six Letters, the Praises of God, the Salutation of the Blessed Virgin, the *Chartula* containing the *Laudes* and Benediction for Brother Leo, the prayer *Absorbeat*, and the Office of the Passion.

The Quaracchi edition does not therefore embody any new matter, but it contains for the first time in any edition of St. Francis' works the letter " To a Minister " in its entirety. For the rest, while purging the text of St. Francis' writings of the many doubtful and apocryphal pieces with which they had come to be burdened in the course of time, the Quaracchi editors have perfected the text of the authentic writings by their emendations and collations, notes and comments, thus conferring the freedom of no small city upon the students of Franciscan sources.

The year 1904 also saw the publication, almost simultaneously, of two other works dealing with the *Opuscula* of St. Francis, written by well-known professors at Bonn[1] and Munich,[2] and both of real value.[3] It would be foreign to our present purpose to examine either of these works in detail. Suffice it to say that they accord in substance almost completely with the conclusions of the Quaracchi editors. If anything, they lean more on the side of kindliness toward certain doubtful writings. Thanks to this trilogy of works, and to certain learned criticisms which they have called forth from Fr. Van

[1] H. Boehmer: *Analekten zur Geschichte des Franciscus von Assisi. S. Francisci Opuscula.* Tübingen and Leipzig, 1904.

[2] W. Goetz: *Die Quellen zur Geschichte des hl. Franciscus von Assisi.* Gotha, 1904. The part of this work dealing with the *Opuscula* already appeared in the *Zeitschrift für Kirchengeschichte.* As there is some difference between the reprint and the original, I have quoted sometimes from one and sometimes from the other.

[3] There is also an excellent new French translation by Fr. Ubald d'Alençon, O.M.Cap.,—*Les Opuscules de Saint François d'Assise* (Paris, Poussielgue, 1905). I have quoted from it elsewhere. A critical Italian edition is in preparation by Fr. Nicolò Dal-Gal, O.F.M., already well known for his contributions to Franciscan history.

Ortroy,[1] M. Sabatier,[2] and Mr. Carmichael[3] among others, we are now in a position to form a fairly accurate estimate of what St. Francis really *wrote*.

It is obvious, however, that in dealing with writings like those of St. Francis we are left largely to the probabilities of criticism; and criticism has by no means said the last word as to the authenticity of certain pieces. It may yet take away from St. Francis some writings now commonly ascribed to him; it may even give back to him others at present with seemingly greater likelihood made over to one or another of his immediate followers. But in the long run, to whatever criticism St. Francis' writings may be subjected, the main lines will always remain the same. It may well be true as a recent writer[4] has remarked, that it is not yet the time to essay a complete English edition of St. Francis' writings, yet withal the lack of any translation of these writings in English which aims at fulfilling the requirements of modern criticism has led me to think that English students of Franciscan literature might be glad to have some such translation of them, however imperfect. To this end I have ventured

---

[1] See *Analecta Bollandiana*, fasc. III, p. 411.

[2] Examen de quelques travaux recents sur les Opuscules de Saint François, in *Opuscules*, fasc. X.

[3] "The Writings of St. Francis," by Montgomery Carmichael, in the *Month*, January, 1904.

[4] See *The Words of St. Francis*, by Anne Macdonell, p. 7, London, 1904.

to prepare this humble volume, which may perhaps be suffered tentatively, at least, to stand in the gap which it is not worthy permanently to fill.

My first object, then, is to give a literal and, I hope, accurate translation of the Latin text of the authentic writings of St. Francis as it stands in the critical Quaracchi edition. The present volume, however, represents something more than a mere translation of the Quaracchi text. In the first place it is not restricted to the Latin works of St. Francis, and as a consequence the "Canticle of the Sun," which does not figure in the Quaracchi edition, finds a place here. I have often deviated from the order of the Quaracchi edition and have distributed the critical notes throughout the book instead of relegating them to the end. I have added an Introduction, Appendix, Bibliography and Index, besides much original matter collected at Quaracchi and elsewhere in Italy, when I was afforded an opportunity of consulting the original MS. authorities. I should state that I have not translated all the variants in the Latin text, but only such as change the sense. A table I had made for the purpose of indicating the probable date of each piece, I have omitted, since it remains a matter of pure conjecture when many were written.

I am glad of this opportunity to record my sincere thanks to all those who have assisted me in any way in the preparation of this volume. Not only have I profited by the labors of the

Fathers at Quaracchi, but I have enjoyed the rare advantage of Fr. Leonard Lemmens' personal interest in the work. To him, therefore, my grateful recognition is first due. I wish further to acknowledge my indebtedness to Mr. Montgomery Carmichael, who, amid his own literary labors, made time to assist me with many helpful suggestions. Moreover, by placing at my disposal all the references to Holy Scripture which occur in the Office of the Passion, which he had looked up and translated, he has afforded me very substantial aid. My thanks are also due to Father Stephen Donovan, O.F.M., for his kind coöperation in collating the text of the "Canticle of the Sun," in the Assisi MS., with other versions, and for contributing the translation of it. For the generous loan of books of reference I am under obligation to Mgr. O'Hare, Father John J. Wynne, S.J., Fathers Ludger Beck, and Bede Oldegeering, O.F.M., and Mr. John A. Tennant; for the gift of their own writings to Father Cuthbert, O.S.F.C., Luigi Suttina, and Prof. A. G. Little; and for the photographs here reproduced to Mgr. Faloci Pulignani, M. Paul Sabatier and Signor Lunghi. I may perhaps be permitted to take this occasion to thank the Guardians at the Portiuncula, La Verna, St.Damian's, and the Carceri, as well as the Friars at St. Antony's and St. Isidore's at Rome, at Ognissanti, Florence, and the Mother Abbess at Santa Chiara, for their courtesy and hospitality.

For the rest, it is with a clear sense of its many shortcomings and not without some diffidence that I offer this volume to the public. I shall be more than repaid for any labor its preparation may have entailed if its publication conduces ever so little toward making St. Francis better known and better loved. To this end I ask the reader to forget all that may be mine within these pages, and to remember only the

words of him who, "saintlier than any among the saints, among sinners was as one of themselves." [1]

FR. PASCHAL ROBINSON, O.F.M.,

Franciscan Convent, Paterson, N. J.
Feast of St. Agnes of Asissi, 1905.

[1] I Cel. 29.

PART I

ADMONITIONS, RULES, ETC

I

WORDS OF ADMONITION OF OUR HOLY FATHER ST. FRANCIS.

NDER this title a precious series of spiritual counsels on the religious life has come down to us from the pen of St. Francis. The early Legends afford no indication of the time or circumstances of the composition of these Admonitions; nor is it possible to determine by whom they were collected. But they accord so completely with the Saint's genuine works and are so redolent of his spirit that their authenticity is admitted by all.[1] Moreover, the various codices in which these Admonitions may be found are unanimous in attributing them to St. Francis, while the number of the Admonitions[2] and the order in which they are given in the different codices are almost the same as in the Laurentian codex at Florence, dating from the thirteenth century.

Codices containing the Admonitions of St. Francis are to be found at the following places : 1. *Assisi* (Munic. lib. cod. 338, fol. 18);—2. *Berlin* (Royal lib. cod. lat. 196, fol. 101);—3. *Florence* (Laurentian lib.

---

[1] See Goetz: Quellen zur Geschichte des hl. Franz von Assisi, in *Zeitschrift für Kirchengeschichte*, t. xxii, p. 551, and Van Ortroy, S.J., in *Anal. Bolland.*, t. xxiv, fasc. iii (1905), p. 411.

[2] The codex of St. Antony's College, Rome, omits the Admonitions numbered 11 and 22. It may be noted, however, that both these numbers are found at the end of the *Speculum Perfectionis*, ed. Lemmens. See *Documenta Antiqua Franciscana*, P. II, p. 84.

cod. X. Plut. XIX. dextr., fol. 448);—4. *Florence* (cod. of the Convent of Ognissanti, fol. 5);—5. *St. Floriano* (monast. lib. cod. XI. 148, fol. 38);—6. *Foligno* (cod. of Capuchin Conv., fol. 21);—7. *Lemberg* (Univ. lib. cod. 131, fol. 331);—8. *Liegnitz*[1] (lib. of SS. Peter and Paul. cod. 12, fol. 131);—9. *Luttich* (Munic. lib. cod. 343, fol. 154);—10. *Munich* (Royal lib. cod. lat. 11354, fol. 25, number 1 only);—11. *Naples* (Nation. lib. cod. XII. F. 32, folio antepaen. numbers 6–27);—12. *Oxford*[2] (Bodl. lib. cod. Canon miscell. 525, fol. 93);—13. *Paris* (Nat. lib. cod. 18327, fol. 154); —14, 15. *Paris* (Mazarin lib. cod. 1743, fol. 134, and cod. 989, fol. 191);—16. *Paris* (codex at lib. of the Prot. theol. faculty, fol. 86);—17. *Prague* (Metrop. lib. cod. B. XC., fol. 244);—18. *Rome* (codex at St. Antony's Coll.,[3] fol. 77);—19, 20. *Rome* (archiv. of St. Isidore's College, cod. 1/25, fol. 14, and cod. 1/73, fol. 11); —21, 22. *Rome* (Vatic. lib. cod. 4354, fol. 39, and cod. 7650, fol. 10);—23. *Toledo* (capit. lib. cod. Cai. 25, no. 11, fol. 65) and—24. *Volterra* (Guarnacci lib. cod. 225, fol. 141).

Of the foregoing codices that in the Laurentian Library at Florence dates from the thirteenth century; those at Ognissanti, Florence, at Assisi, Berlin, St. Floriano, Oxford, Rome (St. Antony's, St. Isidore's, and the Vatican codex 4354), Toledo, and Volterra date from the fourteenth, and the others from the fifteenth century.

For the Quaracchi edition of the Admonitions, upon which the present translation is based, the two oldest of all these codices, to wit, those of the Laurentian

[1] On this MS. see Sabatier, *Opuscules*, fasc. ii.

[2] On this MS. see Little, *Opuscules*, fasc. v.

[3] As to this codex see Lemmens: *Documenta Antiqua Franciscana*, P. III, p. 72.

Library at Florence and of the Municipal Library at Assisi,[1] have been used. Those at St. Isidore's, Rome, and Ognissanti, Florence, have also been consulted, besides the editions of the Admonitions found in the *Monumenta Ordinis Minorum* (Salamanca, 1511, tract. 11, fol. 276 r), the *Firmamenta Trium Ordinum*[2] (Paris, 1512, P. I, fol. 19 r), and the *Liber Conformitatum* of Bartholomew of Pisa (Milan, 1510, fruct. XII, P. 11). But for the titles and paragraphing, which differ more or less in different codices, the Laurentian codex has been followed.[3]

So much by way of preface to the

ADMONITIONS.

1. **Of the Lord's Body.** The Lord Jesus said to His disciples : "I am the Way, and the Truth, and the Life. No man cometh to the Father, but by Me. If you had known Me you would, without doubt, have known My Father also : and from henceforth you shall

---

[1] Mgr. Faloci has edited the first of the Admonitions from this codex in his *Miscellanea Francescana*, t. vi, p. 96.

[2] In this edition, which Wadding has followed (fol. 21 v.), nos. 20, 21, and 23 are repeated.

[3] In places where variants are noted at the foot of the page the following abbreviations will be used:

L.   Laurentian Codex.
As. Assisian Codex.
O.   Ognissanti Codex.
An. Codex at St. Antony's College.
Is. Codex at St. Isidore's College.
Mon. Version of the *Monumenta*.
Firm. Version of the *Firmamenta*.
Pis. Version given by Bartholomew of Pisa in his *Conformities*.

know Him, and you have seen Him. Philip saith
to Him: Lord, show us the Father, and it is enough
for us. Jesus saith to him: Have I been so long
a time with you and have you not known Me?
Philip, he that seeth Me seeth [My] Father also.
How sayest thou, Shew us the Father?"[1]   The
Father "inhabiteth light inaccessible,"[2] and
"God is a spirit,"[3] and "no man hath seen God
at any time."[4] Because God is a spirit, therefore it is only by the spirit He can be seen, for
"it is the spirit that quickeneth; the flesh prof-
iteth nothing."[5] For neither is the Son, inas-
much as He is equal to the Father, seen by any
one other than by the Father, other than by the
Holy Ghost.   Wherefore, all those who saw the
Lord Jesus Christ according to humanity and
did not see and believe according to the Spirit
and the Divinity, that He was the Son of God,
were condemned.   In like manner, all those
who behold the Sacrament of the Body of
Christ which is sanctified by the word of the
Lord upon the altar by the hands of the priest
in the form of bread and wine, and who do not
see and believe according to the Spirit and
Divinity that It is really the most holy Body and
Blood of our Lord Jesus Christ, are condemned,
He the Most High having declared it when He
said, "This is My Body, and the Blood of the
New Testament,"[6] and "he that eateth My

---

[1] John 14: 6–9.
[2] I Tim. 6: 16.
[3] John 4 : 24.
[4] John 1 : 18.
[5] John 6 : 64.
[6] Mark 14 : 22–24.

Flesh and drinketh My Blood hath everlasting life." [1]

Wherefore [he who has][2] the Spirit of the Lord which dwells in His faithful, he it is who receives the most holy Body and Blood of the Lord : all others who do not have this same Spirit and who presume to receive Him, eat and drink judgment to themselves.[3] Wherefore, "O ye sons of men, how long will you be dull of heart ?"[4] Why will you not know the truth and "believe in the Son of God ?"[5] Behold daily He humbles Himself as when from His "royal throne"[6] He came into the womb of the Virgin ; daily He Himself comes to us with like humility ; daily He descends from the bosom of His Father upon the altar in the hands of the priest. And as He appeared in true flesh to the Holy Apostles, so now He shows Himself to us in the sacred Bread ; and as they by means of their fleshly eyes saw only His flesh, yet contemplating Him with their spiritual eyes, believed Him to be God, so we, seeing bread and wine with bodily eyes, see and firmly believe it to be His most holy Body and true and living Blood. And in this way our Lord is ever with His faithful, as He Himself says : "Behold I am with you all days, even to the consummation of the world."[7]

[1] John 6 : 55.
[2] These words are added in the text given by Pis. and Wadd.
[3] See I Cor. 11 : 29.   [4] Ps. 4 : 3.
[5] John 9 : 35.   [6] Wis. 18 : 15.
[7] Matt. 28 : 20.

2. The Evil of Self-will.

The Lord God said to Adam: "Of every tree of paradise thou shalt eat. But of the tree of knowledge of good and evil thou shalt not eat." [1] Adam therefore might eat of every tree of paradise and so long as he did not offend against obedience he did not sin. For one eats of the tree of knowledge of good who appropriates to himself his own will [2] and prides himself upon the goods which the Lord publishes and works in him and thus, through the suggestion of the devil and transgression of the commandment, he finds the apple of the knowledge of evil; wherefore, it behooves that he suffer punishment.

3. Of Perfect and Imperfect Obedience.

The Lord says in the Gospel: he "that doth not renounce all that he possesseth cannot be" a "disciple" [3] and "he that will save his life, shall lose it." [4] That man leaves all he possesses and loses his body and his soul who abandons himself wholly to obedience in the hands of his superior, and whatever he does and says—provided he himself knows that what he does is good and not contrary to his [the superior's] will—is true obedience. And if at times a subject sees things which would be better or more useful to his soul than those which the

---

[1] Gen. 2 : 16-17.

[2] To which, namely, he has no right after religious profession, having relinquished his will by the vow of obedience.

[3] Luke 14 : 33.   [4] Matt. 16 : 25.

superior commands him, let him sacrifice his will to God, let him strive to fulfil the work enjoined by the superior. This is true and charitable obedience which is pleasing to God and to one's neighbor.

If, however, a superior command anything to a subject that is against his soul it is permissible for him to disobey, but he must not leave him [the superior], and if in consequence he suffer persecution from some, he should love them the more for God's sake. For he who would rather suffer persecution than wish to be separated from his brethren, truly abides in perfect obedience because he lays down his life for his brothers.[1] For there are many religious who, under pretext of seeing better things than those which their superiors command, look back[2] and return to the vomit of their own will.[3] These are homicides and by their bad example cause the loss of many souls.

4. That no one should take Superiorship upon himself. I did "not come to be ministered unto, but to minister," says the Lord.[4] Let those who are set above others glory in this superiority only as much as if they had been deputed to wash the feet of the brothers; and if they are more perturbed by the loss of their superiority than they would be by losing the office of washing feet, so much

[1] See John 15 : 13.   [2] See Luke 9 : 62.
[3] See Prov. 26 : 11.   [4] Matt. 20 : 28.

the more do they lay up treasures to the peril of their own soul.

5. **That no one should glory save in the Cross of the Lord.**

Consider, O man, how great the excellence in which the Lord has placed you because He has created and formed you to the image of His beloved Son according to the body and to His own likeness according to the spirit.[1] And all the creatures that are under heaven serve and know and obey their Creator in their own way better than you. And even the demons did not crucify Him, but you together with them crucified Him and still crucify Him by taking delight in vices and sins. Wherefore then can you glory? For if you were so clever and wise that you possessed all science, and if you knew how to interpret every form of language and to investigate heavenly things minutely, you could not glory in all this, because one demon has known more of heavenly things and still knows more of earthly things than all men, although there may be some man who has received from the Lord a special knowledge of sovereign wisdom. In like manner, if you were handsomer and richer than all others, and even if you could work wonders and put the demons to flight, all these things are hurtful to you and in nowise belong to you, and in them you cannot glory; that, however, in which we may glory is in our infirmities,[2] and in

[1] See Gen. 1 : 26.   [2] See II Cor. 12 : 5.

bearing daily the holy cross of our Lord Jesus Christ.

6. Of the Imitation of the Lord.

Let us all, brothers, consider the Good Shepherd who to save His sheep bore the suffering of the Cross. The sheep of the Lord followed Him in tribulation and persecution and shame, in hunger and thirst, in infirmity and temptations and in all other ways;[1] and for these things they have received everlasting life from the Lord. Wherefore it is a great shame for us, the servants of God, that, whereas the Saints have practised works, we should expect to receive honor and glory for reading and preaching the same.

7. That Good Works should accompany Knowledge.

The Apostle says, "the letter killeth, but the spirit quickeneth."[2] They are killed by the letter who seek only to know the words that they may be esteemed more learned among others and that they may acquire great riches to leave to their relations and friends. And those religious are killed by the letter who will not follow the spirit of the Holy Scriptures, but who seek rather to know the words only and to interpret them to others. And they are quickened by the spirit of the Holy Scriptures who do not interpret

[1] See John 10: 11; Heb. 12: 2; John 10: 4; Rom. 8: 35.
[2] II Cor. 3: 6.

materially every text they know or wish to know, but who by word and example give them back to God from whom is all good.

**8. Of avoid-
ing the Sin of**   The Apostle affirms that "no man can say the Lord Jesus but by the Holy Ghost,"[1] and "there is none that doth good, no not one."[2] Whosoever, therefore, envies his brother on account of the good which the Lord says or does in him, commits a sin akin to blasphemy, because he envies the Most High Himself who says and does all that is good.

9. Of Love.   The Lord says in the Gospel, "Love your enemies," etc.[3] He truly loves his enemy who does not grieve because of the wrong done to himself, but who is afflicted for love of God because of the sin on his [brother's] soul and who shows his love by his works.

**10. Of Bodily
Mortification.**   There are many who if they commit sin or suffer wrong often blame their enemy or their neighbor.   But this is not right, for each one has his enemy in his power,—to wit, the body by which he sins.   Wherefore blessed is that servant who always holds captive the enemy

---

[1] I Cor. 12: 3.   [2] Ps. 52: 4.
Matt. 5: 44.

thus given into his power and wisely guards himself from it, for so long as he acts thus no other enemy visible or invisible can do him harm.

11. That one must not be seduced by Bad Example.[1] To the servant of God nothing should be displeasing save sin. And no matter in what way any one may sin, if the servant of God is troubled or angered—except this be through charity—he treasures up guilt to himself.[2] The servant of God who does not trouble himself or get angry about anything lives uprightly and without sin. And blessed is he who keeps nothing for himself, rendering "to Cæsar the things that are Cæsar's and to God the things that are God's."[3]

12. Of Knowing the Spirit of God. Thus may the servant of God know if he has the Spirit of God: if when the Lord works some good through him, his body—since it is ever at variance with all that is good—is not therefore puffed up; but if he rather becomes viler in his own sight and if he esteems himself less than other men.[4]

---

[1] This Admonition is wanting in codex An., but is found in the *Speculum Perfectionis*, ed. Lemmens. See *Documenta Antiqua Franciscana*, P. II, p. 84.

[2] See Rom. 2 : 5.   [3] Matt. 22 : 21.

[4] Cod. O. and Is. read: "If therefore his body is puffed up, he has not the Spirit of God. If, however, he becomes rather viler in his own sight, then he truly has the Spirit of God."

13. 𝔒𝔣 𝔓𝔞
𝔱𝔦𝔢𝔫𝔠𝔢.   How much interior patience and humility a servant of God may have cannot be known so long as he is contented.[1] But when the time comes that those who ought to please him go against him, as much patience and humility as he then shows, so much has he and no more.

14. 𝔒𝔣 𝔓𝔬𝔟
𝔢𝔯𝔱𝔶 𝔬𝔣 𝔖𝔭𝔦𝔯𝔦𝔱.   " Blessed are the poor in spirit : for theirs is the kingdom of heaven."[2] Many apply themselves to prayers and offices, and practise much abstinence and bodily mortification, but because of a single word which seems to be hurtful to their bodies or because of something being taken from them, they are forthwith scandalized and troubled. These are not poor in spirit : for he who is truly poor in spirit, hates himself and loves those who strike him on the cheek.[3]

15. 𝔒𝔣 𝔓𝔢𝔞𝔠𝔢
𝔪𝔞𝔨𝔢𝔯𝔰.   " Blessed are the peacemakers : for they shall be called the children of God."[4] They are truly peacemakers who amidst all they suffer in this world maintain peace in soul and body for the love of our Lord Jesus Christ.

---

[1] Cod. O. reads : " so long as he enjoys everything according to his wish and necessity."

[2] Matt. 5 : 3.   [3] See Matt. 5 : 39.

[4] Matt. 5 : 9.

16. Of Cleanness of Heart. " Blessed are the clean of heart : for they shall see God."[1] They are clean of heart who despise earthly things and always seek those of heaven, and who never cease to adore and contemplate the Lord God Living and True, with a pure heart and mind.

17. Of the Humble Servant of God. Blessed is that servant who is not more puffed up because of the good the Lord says and works through him than because of that which He says and works through others. A man sins who wishes to receive more from his neighbor than he is himself willing to give to the Lord God.

18. Of Compassion toward one's Neighbor. Blessed is the man who bears with his neighbor according to the frailty of his nature as much as he would wish to be borne with by him if he should be in a like case.

19. Of the Happy and Unhappy Servant. Blessed is the servant who gives up all his goods to the Lord God, for he who retains anything for himself hides " his Lord's money,"[2] and that " which he thinketh he hath shall be taken away from him."[3]

[1] Matt. 5: 8.   [2] See Matt. 25 : 18.
[3] Luke 8 : 18.

20. Of the Good and Humble Religious. Blessed is the servant who does not regard himself as better when he is esteemed and extolled by men than when he is reputed as mean, simple, and despicable : for what a man is in the sight of God, so much he is, and no more.[1]   Woe to that religious who is elevated in dignity by others, and who of his own will is not ready to descend.   And blessed is that servant who is raised in dignity not by his own will and who always desires to be beneath the feet of others.

21. Of the Happy and the Vain Religious. Blessed is that religious who feels no pleasure or joy save in most holy conversation and the works of the Lord, and who by these means leads men[2] to the love of God in joy and gladness.   And woe to that religious who takes delight in idle and vain words and by this means provokes men to laughter.

22. Of the Frivolous and Talkative Religious.[3] Blessed is that servant who does not speak through hope of reward and who does not manifest everything and is not "hasty to speak,"[4] but who

---

[1] See Bonav. *Leg. Maj.*, VI, 1: "And he had these words continually in his mouth : ' what a man is in the eyes of God, so much he is, and no more. ' " See also *Imitation of Christ*, Bk. III, Chap. L, where the same saying of St. Francis is quoted.

[2] See *Speculum Perfectionis*, ed. Sabatier, p. 189.

[3] This Admonition (like No. 11) is wanting in Cod. An., but is found in the *Speculum Perfectionis*, ed. Lemmens.   See *Doc. Ant. Franc.*, P. II, p. 84.

[4] Prov. 29 : 20.

wisely foresees what he ought to say and answer. Woe to that religious who not concealing in his heart the good things which the Lord has disclosed to him and who not manifesting them to others by his work, seeks rather through hope of reward to make them known to men by words: for now he receives his recompense and his hearers bear away little fruit.

23. **Of True Correction.** Blessed is the servant who bears discipline, accusation, and blame from others as patiently as if they came from himself. Blessed is the servant who, when reproved, mildly submits, modestly obeys, humbly confesses, and willingly satisfies. Blessed is the servant who is not prompt to excuse himself and who humbly bears shame and reproof for sin when he is without fault.

24. **Of True Humility.**[1] Blessed is he[2] who shall be found as humble among his subjects as if he were among his masters. Blessed is the servant who always continues under the rod of correction. He is "a faithful and wise servant"[3] who does not delay to punish himself for all his offences, interiorly by contrition and exteriorly by confession and by works of satisfaction.

---

[1] In Cod. O. numbers 23 and 24 are not divided.
[2] Cod. An. reads: "Blessed is that superior
[3] Matt. 24: 45.

26. Of True Love.

Blessed is that brother who would love his brother as much when he is ill and not able to assist him as he loves him when he is well and able to assist him. Blessed is the brother who would love and fear his brother as much when he is far from him as he would when with him, and who would not say anything about him behind his back that he could not with charity say in his presence.

26. That the Servants of God should honor Clerics.

Blessed is the servant of God who exhibits confidence in clerics who live uprightly according to the form of the holy Roman Church. And woe to those who despise them : for even though they [the clerics] may be sinners, nevertheless no one ought to judge them, because the Lord Himself reserves to Himself alone the right of judging them. For as the administration with which they are charged, to wit, of the most holy Body and Blood of our Lord Jesus Christ, which they receive and which they alone administer to others—is greater than all others, even so the sin of those who offend against them is greater than any against all the other men in this world.

27. Of the Virtues putting Vices to flight.

Where there is charity and wisdom there is neither fear nor ignorance. Where there is patience and humility there is neither anger nor worry.[1] Where there is poverty and joy there is neither cupidity nor avarice. Where there is quiet and meditation there is neither solicitude nor dissipation. Where there is the fear of the Lord to guard the house the enemy cannot find a way to enter. Where there is mercy and discretion there is neither superfluity nor hard-heartedness.

28. Of hiding Good lest it be lost.

Blessed is the servant who treasures up in heaven[2] the good things which the Lord shows him and who does not wish to manifest them to men through the hope of reward, for the Most High will Himself manifest his works to whomsoever He may please. Blessed is the servant who keeps the secrets of the Lord in his heart.[3]

[1] Cod. O. omits this sentence.

[2] See Matt. 6 : 20.

[3] St. Francis would often say to his brethren : " When a servant of God receives any divine inspiration in prayer, he ought to say, ' This consolation, O Lord, Thou hast sent from heaven to me, a most unworthy sinner, and I commit it to Thy care, for I know that I should be but a thief of Thy treasure.' And when he returns to prayer, he ought to bear himself as a little one and a sinner, as if he had received no new grace from God."—St. Bonaventure, *Leg. Maj.*, X, 4.

II.
SALUTATION OF THE VIRTUES.

Thomas of Celano, St. Francis' earliest biographer, bears witness to the authenticity of this exquisite Salutation in his *Second Life*, written about 1247.[1] It is found in the codices of Assisi, Berlin, Florence (Ognissanti MS.), Foligno, Liegnitz, Naples, Paris (Mazarin MSS. and MS. of Prot. theol. fac.), and Rome (Vatican MSS.), above mentioned,[2] as well as at Düsseldorf (Royal arch. cod. B. 132), and is given by Bartholomew of Pisa in his *Liber Conformitatum*[3] (fruct. XII, P. 11, Cap. 38). This Salutation was also published in the *Speculum Vitae B. Francisci et Sociorum Ejus* (fol. 126 v)[4] and by Wadding,[5] who followed the Assisian codex. This codex, which is the oldest one containing the Salutation, has been used for the Quaracchi edition, which I have here followed, as well as the Ognissanti MS. and the version given in the *Conformities*.

Now follows the

SALUTATION OF THE VIRTUES.[6]

Hail,[7] queen wisdom! May the Lord save thee with thy sister holy pure simplicity! O

---

[1] "Wherefore," he writes of St. Francis, "in the praises of the virtues which he composed he says 'Hail! queen wisdom, God save Thee with Thy sister pure, holy simplicity.'" See *2 Cel.* 3, 119, for this *Incipit*.

[2] See page 3.

[3] In the text of the *Conformities* (which for the most part agrees with that of the Ognissanti MS.) the Salutation is preceded by No. 27 of the Admonitions and begins with the words "There is absolutely no man," etc.

[4] Ed. of Venice, 1504, and of Metz, 1509.

[5] *Opuscula*, Antwerp, 1623.

[6] In the Assisi codex (as in that of Liegnitz) the title reads: (*Notes 6 and 7 carried forward to next page.*)

Lady, holy poverty, may the Lord save thee with thy sister holy humility! O Lady, holy charity, [may the Lord save thee with thy sister holy obedience! O all ye most holy virtues, may the Lord, from whom you proceed and come, save you! There is absolutely no man in the whole world who can possess one among you unless he first die. He who possesses one and does not offend the others, possesses all; and he who offends one, possesses none and offends all; and every one [of them] confounds vices and sins. Holy wisdom confounds Satan and all his wickednesses. Pure holy simplicity confounds all the wisdom of this world and the wisdom of the flesh. Holy poverty confounds cupidity and avarice and the cares of this world. Holy humility confounds pride and all the men of this world and all things that are in the world. Holy charity confounds all diabolical and fleshly temptations and all fleshly fears. Holy obedience confounds all bodily and fleshly desires and keeps the body mortified to the obedience of the spirit and to the obedience of one's brother and makes a man subject to all the men of this world and not to men alone, but also to all beasts and wild animals, so that they may do with him whatsoever they will, in so far as it may be granted to them from above by the Lord.

"Of the virtues with which the Blessed Virgin Mary was adorned and with which a holy soul ought also to be adorned," whereas in the Ognissanti codex and others of the same class, the title is: "Salutation of the Virtues and of their efficacy in confounding Vice." (See Introduction.)

⁷ Cod. As. omits " Hail."

III.

ON REVERENCE FOR THE LORD'S BODY AND ON THE CLEANLINESS OF THE ALTAR.

The arguments already adduced to establish the authenticity of the Admonitions may also be used in behalf of this instruction addressed "to all clerics." It is found in eight of the codices above mentioned—to wit, those of Assisi, Liegnitz, Paris (both Mazarin MSS. and at lib. of Prot. theol. fac.), Rome (St. Antony's and St. Isidore's MS. ⅛₃), and Düsseldorf. In Wadding's edition of the *Opuscula* this instruction on the Blessed Sacrament is placed among the letters of St. Francis[1] (No. XIII), but the early codices do not give it in an epistolary form,[2] but rather as it is printed here without address or salutation. For the present edition the Assisian codex[3] has

---

[1] Wadding, following Mariano of Florence, prefaces the letter with the following Salutation: "To my reverend masters in Christ; to all the clerics who are in the world and live conformably to the rules of the Catholic faith: brother Francis, their least one and unworthy servant, sends greeting with the greatest respect and kissing their feet. Since I am become the servant of all, but cannot, on account of my infirmities, address you personally and *viva voce*, I beg you to receive, with all love and charity, this remembrance of me and exhortation which I write briefly." Wadding also (p. 45) adds at the end of this instruction the following words: "May our Lord Jesus Christ fill all my masters with His holy grace and comfort them."

[2] Father Ubald d'Alençon (*Opuscules de Saint François*, p. 21) is inclined, with M. Sabatier, to regard this instruction as a kind of postscript to St. Francis' letter to the General Chapter and to all the Friars. (See *Speculum Perfectionis*, ed. Sabatier, p. clxvi.)

[3] Mgr. Faloci has edited the Instruction after this codex; see *Misc. Francescana*, t. VI, p. 95.

been used as well as the codices of St. Antony's and St. Isidore's at Rome. The text is as follows :

ON REVERENCE FOR THE LORD'S BODY AND ON THE CLEANLINESS OF THE ALTAR.

Let us all consider, O clerics, the great sin and ignorance of which some are guilty regarding the most holy Body and Blood of our Lord Jesus Christ and His most holy Name and the written words of consecration. For we know that the Body cannot exist until after these words of consecration. For we have nothing and we see nothing of the Most High Himself in this world except [His] Body and Blood, names and words by which we have been created and redeemed from death to life.

But let all those who administer such most holy mysteries, especially those who do so indifferently, consider among themselves how poor the chalices, corporals, and linens may be where the Body and Blood of our Lord Jesus Christ is sacrificed. And by many It is left in wretched places and carried by the way disrespectfully, received unworthily and administered to others indiscriminately. Again His Names and written words are sometimes trampled under foot, for the sensual man perceiveth not these things that are of God.[1] Shall we not by all these things be moved with a sense of duty when the good Lord Himself places Himself in our hands and we handle Him and receive Him daily?

[1] See I Cor. 2: 14.

Are we unmindful that we must needs fall into His hands?

Let us then at once and resolutely correct these faults and others; and wheresoever the most holy Body of our Lord Jesus Christ may be improperly reserved and abandoned, let It be removed thence and let It be put and enclosed in a precious place. In like manner wheresoever the Names and written words of the Lord may be found in unclean places they ought to be collected and put away in a decent place. And we know that we are bound above all to observe all these things by the commandments of the Lord and the constitutions of holy Mother Church. And let him who does not act thus know that he shall have to render an account therefor before our Lord Jesus Christ on the day of judgment. And let him who may cause copies of this writing to be made, to the end that it may be the better observed, know that he is blessed by the Lord.

IV.

RULES OF THE FRIARS MINOR.

The early history of the Seraphic legislation, to wit, the Rules of the Friars Minor, the Poor Ladies and the Brothers and Sisters of Penance, is intricate beyond measure, as those at all conversant with the subject are but too well aware. Withal, as regards the Rule of the Friars Minor, with which we are now more particularly concerned, St. Francis seems, on the whole, to have written it twice. We have the formal testimony of St. Bonaventure and other trustworthy authorities to this effect. Suffice it to say that in the third year after he underwent the great spiritual crisis we call conversion, "the servant of Christ, seeing that the number of his Friars was gradually increasing, wrote for himself and for them a form of life in simple words, laying as its irremovable foundation the observance of the holy Gospel and adding a few other things which seemed necessary for uniformity of life." [1] It was this "form of life," which has become known as the first Rule, that Innocent III approved *viva voce*, April 23, 1209.[2] Some fourteen years later on, when the Order had greatly increased,

[1] See Bonav. *Leg. Maj.*, III, 8. See also 1 Cel. 1, 5, and the *Vita S. Francisci*, by Julian of Spires, cap. iv.

[2] Although M. Sabatier (*Vie de S. François*, p. 100), following Wadding (*Annales* ad an. 1210, n. 220 seq.), fixes this event in the summer of 1210, it is far more probable that the approbation of the Rule took place on April 23, 1209, the date given by the Bollandists and the Seraphic Breviary. This latter date is not only more conformable to the ancient tradition of the Order (see *Anal. Franciscana*, t. III, p. 713) but involves no historic difficulties (see *Appunti critici sulla cronologia della Vita di S. Francesco*, by Father Leo Patrem, O.F.M., in the *Oriente Serafico*, Assisi, 1895, Vol. vii, nn. 4-12.

Francis " desiring to bring *into a shorter form* the Rule handed down in which the words of the Gospel were scattered somewhat diffusely . . . caused a Rule to be written. . . . And this Rule . . . he committed to the keeping of his Vicar, who, after a few days had elapsed, declared that he had carelessly lost it. Once more the holy man . . . rewrote the Rule as at the first . . . and by Pope Honorius obtained its confirmation " [1] on November 29, 1223. Such in briefest outline is the genesis of the first and second Rules written by St. Francis for the Friars Minor.

To these two Rules Prof. Karl Müller[2] and M. Paul Sabatier[3] would fain add a third, written, as they aver, in 1221. Their opinion, however, seems to rest upon a misconception, for the Rule which they describe as dating from 1221, is not a new one, but the same that Innocent III approved, not indeed in its original form, which has not come down to us,[4] but rather in the form it had assumed in the course of twelve years, as a consequence of many changes and additions.[5]

[1] See Bonav. *Leg. Maj.*, IV, 11.

[2] Müller: *Anfänge des Minoriten-Ordens und der Buss-brüderschaften* (Freiburg, 1885), p. 4, seq.

[3] Sabatier : *Vie de S. François d'Assise* (Paris, 1894), p. 288, seq.

[4] More than a century ago—in 1768—Fr. Suyskens demonstrated that the lengthy Rule of twenty-three chapters could not have been presented to Pope Innocent by St. Francis in its present form. (See *Acta S. S.*, t. ii, Oct.) All agree that the first Rule in its original form was very short and simple.

[5] Prof. Müller was therefore right in attempting to reconstruct the Rule in its original form out of this longer one. He has almost conclusively demonstrated that the opening words of this original Rule were: " Regula et vita istorum fratrum haec est." (See *Anfänge*, pp. 14-25 ; 185-188.) Prof. Boehmer has also attempted to reconstruct it from various writings. See his *Analekten*, p. 27. See also 2 Cel. 3, 110 ; *Speculum Perfectionis* (ed. Sabatier), c. 4, n. 42.

Early expositors of the Rule, such as Hugo de Digne[1] and Angelo Clareno,[2] in their works always represent the Rule of which we are now speaking as the first and original one. Moreover, none of the thirteenth century writers make mention of any third rule; they speak only of the changes and accretions which the first Rule suffered between 1209 and 1223.[3]

For example Jordan a Giano tells us that St. Francis chose Brother Cæsar of Spires, a profound student of Scripture and a devoted friend, to assist

[1] His exposition of the Rule may be found in the *Monumenta Ordinis Minorum* (Salamanca, 1511, tract. II, fol. 46 v) and in the *Firmamenta* (Paris, 1512, p. iv, fol. 34 v). In chapter 6 (*Mon.*, fol. 67 v; *Firm.*, fol. 48 r) he says: "This he lays down at greater length in the *original rule* as follows: 'When it may be necessary let the friars go for alms,'" etc. (see below, p. 43). On Hugo de Digne see Sbaralea, *Supplementum*, p. 360; also Salimbene, *Chron. Parmensis*, 1857, *passim*.

[2] His exposition of the Rule has never been published, although a critical edition is promised by Fr. Van Ortroy, S.J. (See *Anal. Bolland.*, t. xxi, p. 441 seq.) Meanwhile it may be found at St. Isidore's, Rome, in the codex ⅓₂; at the Vatican lib., in cod. Ottob. 522 (in part only) and Ottob. 666, and at the Royal lib. of Munich in cod. 23648. In this exposition Clareno says (cod. Ottob. 666, fol. 50 v): "In the Rule which Pope Innocent conceded to him and approved . . . it was written thus: 'The Lord commands in the Gospel,'" etc. (see below, p. 41). Clareno died in 1337. On his writings see Fr. Ehrle, S.J., in the *Archiv*, vol. I (1885), pp. 509–69.

[3] To be sure, the traditional *Legend of the Three Companions* says of St. Francis: "He made many rules and tried them, before he made that which at the last he left to the brothers." (See *Legenda III Sociorum*, n. 35.) But unless these words are understood as referring to different versions of the same Rule, they only raise a new difficulty against the authenticity of this Legend.

him in putting this Rule into shape,[1] and Jacques de Vitry; writing about 1217, relates that the Friars " meet once a year . . . and then with the help of good men adopt and promulgate holy institutions approved by the Pope."[2] One of these institutions has been recorded for us by Thomas of Celano in his *Second Life.* It appears that " on account of a general commotion in a certain chapter, St. Francis caused these words to be written : ' Let the friars take care not to appear gloomy and sad like hypocrites, but let them be jovial and merry, showing that they rejoice in the Lord, and becomingly courteous,' "[3] words which may be found in the seventh chapter of the first Rule.[4] Honorius III, on September 22, 1220, issued a decree forbidding the Friars to leave the Order after having made profession, or to roam about ''beyond the bounds of obedience,'' and this ordinance was added to the second chapter of the Rule.[5]

All permanent and powerful rules *grow*, as a recent writer[6] has justly remarked, and it was thuswise that

---

[1] "And the Blessed Francis seeing Brother Cæsar learned in the Scriptures commissioned him to embellish with evangelical language the Rule which he himself had put together in simple words." *Chron. Fr. Jordani a Jano: Analecta Franc.*, t. I, page 6, n. 15.   Brother Jordan also notes " that according to the first Rule the Friars fasted on Wednesday and Friday." (*L. c.*, p. 4, n. 11.)

[2] See *Speculum Perfectionis* (ed. Sabatier), Appendix, p. 300; also *Les Nouveaux mémoires de l'Académie de Bruxelles*, t. XXIII, pp. 29–33. Jacques de Vitry died as Cardinal Bishop of Frascati in 1244, leaving a number of writings in which St. Francis figures prominently.

[3] 2 Cel., 3, 90.   [4] See below, p. 41.

[5] See below, p. 34.

[6] Canon Knox Little: *St. Francis of Assisi* (1904), Appendix, p. 321.

the first Rule of the Friars Minor received constant additions in the form of constitutions enacted at the Chapters held at Portiuncula after 1212 or otherwise —it is necessary to insist on this point[1]—during the fourteen years it was in force. It is not hard therefore to understand why the texts we have of this Rule do not always agree, since these changes and additions did not come to the knowledge of all through the same channel. For example, in the tenth chapter, which deals with "the sick brothers," we have two different readings: the one followed in the present translation is that found in the majority of the codices;[2] the other, which has been incorporated by Celano in his *Second Life*,[3] has been used by Hugo de Digne in his exposition of the Rule.[4] So too in the twelfth chapter, which prescribes that the friars should avoid the company of women, we find the following addition in the exposition of Angelo Clareno[5] and the *Speculum Vitae B. Francisci*:[6] "Let no one walk abroad with them alone or eat out of the same plate with them at table,"—words not to be found in the more common form of the Rule.

It remains to say a word about the relation of this first Rule to the second and definitive one approved in 1223. In treating of the difference between these two Rules, M. Sabatier errs still more strangely. They had little in common, he avers, except the name, the second being the very antithesis of the first, which alone was truly Franciscan.[7] To say the truth

[1] See Van Ortroy, S.J., *Annal. Bolland.*, t. xxiv, fasc. iii, 1905, p. 413.
[2] See below, p. 44.   [3] See 2 Cel., 3, 110.
[4] See *Mon.*, fol. 68 v; *Firm.*, fol. 49 r.
[5] See Cod. Ottob. 666, fol. 99 v.
[6] See *Speculum*, fol. 193 v.
[7] "Celle de 1210 et celle qui fut approuvée par le pape le

this assertion is less conformable to reality than it is
to the theories and prejudices of the French writer.
In so far as the first and second Rules written by St.
Francis for the Friars Minor may be said to differ,
the difference lies in this that the second Rule is
shorter, more precise, and more orderly;[1] but essen-
tially and in substance it is clearly and truly the
same as the first Rule. Indeed, the very wording of
the second Rule already exists in great part in the
first one, as any one must observe who makes an
unbiassed comparison of the two. So true is this
agreement between the two Rules that they are often
regarded as one and the same. Thus Pope Honorius
III himself in his bull of 1223 confirming the second
Rule makes no distinction between the two. "We
confirm," he says, "the Rule of your Order approved
by Pope Innocent, our predecessor, of happy memory."[2] And Brother Elias, in a letter addressed to
the friars "living near Valenciennes," exhorts them
to observe purely, inviolably, unweariedly the "holy
Rule approved by Pope Innocent and confirmed by
Pope Honorius."[3] Rightly then does Hugo de Digne
("*spiritualis homo ultra modum*") describe the difference between the two Rules in his Exposition,[4]

---

29 Novembre, 1223," he writes, "n'avaient guère de commun
que le nom." . . . "Celle de 1210 seule est vraiment
franciscaine. Celle de 1223 est indirectement l'œuvre de
l'Église."—*Vie de S. François*, p. 289.

[1] See Le Monnier: *History of St. Francis*, p. 337.

[2] See *Seraphicæ Legislationis Textus Originales* (Quaracchi, 1897), p. 35.

[3] This letter, which is dated "in the tenth year of the Pontifi-
cate of Pope Honorius," may be found in the *Annalibus
Hannoniæ Fr. Jacobi de Guisia*, lib. XXI, cap. xvii; see
Monumenta Germaniæ Historica, Scriptores, t. XXX, P. I,
p. 294.

[4] See *Mon.*, fol. 46 v ; *Firm.*, fol. 34 v.

when he says : ." Some things were afterwards omitted
for the sake of brevity from the Rule approved by
Pope Innocent before it was confirmed by the bull of
Pope Honorius. " [1]

For the rest, M. Sabatier's assertion that the
"Spiritual" friars at the beginning of the fourteenth century did not dream of using the first Rule[2],
can hardly be admitted. To refute it, it suffices to
cite Angelo Clareno, the leader of the "Spiritual"
friars, who so very often mentions the first Rule in
his exposition and whose citations prove that in the
first quarter of the fourteenth century there was no
memory of any other Rule, even in the camp of the
rigorists. In a word, "the opposition which the dis-
tinguished French critic would fain set up between
the two Rules, does not exist, and Chapter XV of
his *Life of St. Francis* is not at all consonant with
history." Such is the assertion of the Quaracchi editors. Its truth will be best demonstrated by an
examination of the text of both Rules, which now
follow:

FIRST RULE OF THE FRIARS MINOR

*Which St. Francis made and which Pope Inno-
cent III confirmed without a Bull.*[3]

In the Name of the Father and of the Son
and of the Holy Ghost. Amen. This is the

[1] See Ehrle : "Controversen über die Anfänge des Minoritenordens" in the *Zeitschrift für Katholische Theologie*,
t. XI, p. 725, seq.

[2] "À partir de Bonaventure," he writes, " la règle primitive
tombe dans l'oubli. Les Franciscaines Spirituels du com-
mencement du XIV siècle ne songèrent pas à l'en tirer." See
Spec. Perf. (ed. Sab.), p. ix.

[3] In preparing the Quaracchi text, which is the one I translate here, the codices at St. Antony's and St. Isidore's, and

life that Brother Francis begged might be conceded to him and confirmed by the Lord Pope
Innocent.   And he [the Pope] has conceded and
confirmed it to him and to his brothers present
and future.

Brother Francis, and whoever may be at the
head of this religion, promises obedience and
reverence to our Lord Pope Innocent and to his
successors.   And the other brothers shall be
bound to obey Brother Francis and his successors.[1]

1.—That the Brothers ought to live in Obedience, without Property and in Chastity.

The Rule and life of these brothers is this :
namely, to live in obedience and chastity, and
without property, and to follow the doctrine and
footsteps of our Lord Jesus Christ, who says :
" If thou wilt be perfect, go sell what thou hast,
and give to the poor, and thou shalt have treasure in heaven, and come, follow Me."[2]   And :
" If any man will come after Me, let him deny
himself and take up his cross and follow Me ; "[3]

the Florentine codex at Ognissanti were used, besides the
versions of this Rule found in the *Speculum, Minorum,
Monumenta*, and *Firmamenta* (see Introduction for description of these codices and editions).   The expositions of the
Rule by Hugo de Digne and Angelo Clareno, already mentioned, have often been consulted, as well as the *Conformities* of Bartholomew of Pisa.   The text of the first Rule,
given in part in the *Conformities*, often agrees with the
MSS. of Ognissanti and St. Isidore's.

[1] This last sentence is omitted in *Mon.* and *Firm.*, also by
Wadding.

[2] Matt. 19 : 21.   [3] Matt. 16 : 24.

in like manner : " If any man come to Me, and hate not his father, and mother, and wife, and children, and brethren and sisters, yea, and his own life also, he cannot be My disciple."[1] " And everyone that hath left father or mother, brothers or sisters, or wife, or children or lands, for My sake, shall receive an hundredfold, and shall possess life everlasting." [2]

2.—*Of the Reception and Clothing of the Brothers.*

If any one, wishing by divine inspiration to embrace this manner of life, comes to our brothers, let him be kindly received by them. And if he be firmly resolved to undertake our life, let the brothers take great care ，not to meddle with his temporal affairs, but let them present him as soon as possible to their minister. Let the minister receive him kindly, and encourage him, and diligently explain to him the tenor of our life. This being done, if he be willing and able, with safety of conscience and without impediment, let him sell all his goods and endeavor to distribute them to the poor. But let the brothers and the ministers of the brothers be careful not to interfere in any way in his affairs, and let them not receive any money, either themselves or through any person acting as intermediary ; if however they should be in want, the brothers may accept other necessaries for the body, money excepted, by reason of their necessity, like other poor. And when he [the

[1] Luke 14 : 26.　　　　[2] See Matt. 19 : 29.

candidate] shall have returned, let the minister grant him the habit of probation for a year; that is to say, two tunics without a hood and cord and breeches and a chaperon[1] reaching to the girdle. The year of probation being finished, let him be received to obedience. Afterwards it shall not be lawful for him to pass to another Order, nor to "wander about beyond obedience," according to the commandment of the Lord Pope.[2] For according to the Gospel "no man putting his hand to the plough, and looking back, is fit for the kingdom of God."[3] If, however, anyone should present himself who cannot without difficulty give away his goods, but has the spiritual will to relinquish them, it shall suffice. No one shall be received contrary to the form and institution of the holy Church.

But the other brothers who have promised obedience may have one tunic with a hood, and another without a hood, if necessity require it, and a cord and breeches. And let all the brothers be clothed with mean garments, and they may mend them with sackcloth and other pieces, with the blessing of God, for the Lord says in the Gospel : they that are in costly apparel and live delicately and they that are clothed in soft garments are in the houses of kings.[4] And although they should be called hypocrites, let

---

[1] From the Latin *caparo*. See Du Cange, *Glossar. latin.*

[2] See the bull *Cum secundum* of Honorius III, dated September 22, 1220 (*Bullarium Franciscanum*, t. 1, p. 6.)

[3] Luke 9: 62.   [4] See Matt. 11 : 8; Luke 7 : 25.

them not cease to do good; let them not desire rich clothes in this world, that they may possess a garment in the kingdom of heaven.

3.—*Of the Divine Office and of the Fast.*

The Lord says : "This kind [of devil] can go out by nothing but by fasting and prayer ";[1] and again : "When you fast be not as the hypocrites, sad."[2] For this reason let all the brothers, whether clerics or laics, say the Divine Office, the praises and prayers which they ought to say. The clerics shall say the Office, and say it for the living and the dead, according to the custom of clerics; but to satisfy for the defect and negligence of the brothers, let them say every day *Miserere mei*, with the *Pater noster;* for the deceased brothers let them say *De profundis,* with *Pater noster.* And they may have only the books necessary to perform their Office; and the lay-brothers who know how to read the Psalter may also have one; but the others who do not know how to read may not have a book. The lay-brothers however shall say : *Credo in Deum*, and twenty-four *Paternosters* with *Gloria Patri* for Matins, but for Lauds, five; for Prime, Tierce, Sext, and Nones, for each, seven *Pater-nosters* with *Gloria Patri;* for Vespers, twelve; for Compline, *Credo in Deum* and seven *Pater-nosters* with *Gloria Patri;* for the dead, seven *Paternosters* with *Requiem aeternam;* and for

---

[1] See Mark 9: 28.   [2] Matt. 6: 16.

the defect and negligence of the brothers, three
Paternosters every day.

And all the brothers shall likewise fast from
the feast of All Saints until the Nativity of
our Lord, and from Epiphany, when our Lord
Jesus Christ began to fast, until Easter; but at
other times let them not be bound to fast according to this life except on Fridays. And they
may eat of all foods which are placed before
them, according to the Gospel.[1]

4.—*Of the Ministers and the other Brothers: how they shall be ranged.*

In the Name of the Lord let all the brothers
who are appointed ministers and servants of the
other brothers place their brothers in the prov-
inces or places where they may be, and let them
often visit and spiritually admonish and console
them. And let all my other blessed brothers diligently obey them in those things which look to
the salvation of the soul and are not contrary to
our life. Let them observe among themselves
what the Lord says: "Whatsoever you would
that men should do to you, do you also to them,"[2]
and "what you do not wish done to you, do it not
to others."[3] And let the ministers and servants
remember that the Lord says: I have not "come
to be ministered unto, but to minister,"[4] and
that to them is committed the care of the souls
of their brothers, of whom, if any should be lost

[1] See Luke 10: 8.   [2] Matt. 7: 12.
[3] See Tob. 4: 6.   [4] Matt. 20: 28.

through their fault and bad example, they will have to give an account before the Lord Jesus Christ in the day of judgment.

5.—*Of the Correction of the Brothers who offend.*

Therefore take care of your souls and of those of your brothers, for " it is a fearful thing to fall into the hands of the living God."[1] If however one of the ministers should command some one of the brothers anything contrary to our life or against his soul, the brother is not bound to obey him, because that is not obedience in which a fault or sin is committed. Nevertheless, let all the brothers who are subject to the ministers and servants consider reasonably and carefully the deeds of the ministers and servants. And if they should see any one of them walking according to the flesh and not according to the spirit, according to the right way of our life, after the third admonition, if he will not amend, let him be reported to the minister and servant of the whole fraternity in the Whitsun Chapter, in spite of any obstacle that may stand in the way. If however among the brothers, wherever they may be, there should be some brother who desires to live according to the flesh, and not according to the spirit, let the brothers with whom he is admonish, instruct, and correct him humbly and diligently. And if after the third admonition he will not amend, let them as soon as possible send him, or make the matter known to his

[1] Ieb. 10: 31.

minister and servant, and let the minister and
servant do with him what may seem to him most
expedient before God.

And let all the brothers, the ministers and
servants as well as the others, take care not to
be troubled or angered because of the fault or
bad example of another, for the devil desires to
corrupt many through the sin of one; but let
them spiritually help him who has sinned, as best
they can; for he that is whole needs not a physician, but he that is sick.[1]

In like manner let not all the brothers have
power and authority, especially among themselves, for as the Lord says in the Gospel: "The
princes of the Gentiles lord it over them: and
they that are the greater exercise power upon
them."[2] It shall not be thus among the brothers,
but whosoever will be the greater among them,
let him be their minister and servant,[3] and he
that is the greater among them let him be as
the younger,[4] and he who is the first, let him be
as the last.   Let not any brother do evil or
speak evil to another; let them rather in the
spirit of charity willingly serve and obey each
other: and this is the true and holy obedience
of our Lord Jesus Christ.   And let all the brothers as often soever as they may have declined
from the commandments of God, and wandered
from obedience, know that, as the prophet says,[5]

---

[1] See Matt. 9: 12.   Matt. 20: 25.
[2] See Matt. 23: 11.   [4] See Luke 22: 26.
  See Ps. 118: 21.

they are cursed out of obedience as long as they
continue consciously in such a sin. And when
they persevere in the commandments of the
Lord, which they have promised by the holy
Gospel and their life, let them know that they
abide in true obedience, and are blessed by God.

6.—*Of the Recourse of the Brothers to their Ministers and that no Brother may be called Prior.*

Let the brothers, in whatsoever places they
may be, if they cannot observe our life, have
recourse as soon as possible to their minister,
making this known to him. But let the minister
endeavor to provide for them in such a way as he
would wish to be dealt with himself if he were in
the like case. And let no one be called Prior,
but let all in general be called Friars Minor.
And let one wash the feet of the other.

7.—*Of the Manner of serving and working.*

Let the brothers in whatever places they may
be among others to serve or to work, not be
chamberlains, nor cellarers, nor overseers in the
houses of those whom they serve, and let them
not accept any employment which might cause
scandal, or be injurious to their soul,[1] but let
them be inferior and subject to all who are in
the same house.

And let the brothers who know how to work,
labor and exercise themselves in that art they
may understand, if it be not contrary to the

[1] See Mark 8 : 36.

salvation of their soul, and they can exercise it becomingly. For the prophet says : " For thou shalt eat the labors of thy hands; blessed art thou, and it shall be well with thee " ; [1] and the Apostle : " If any man will not work, neither let him eat." [2] And let every man abide in the art or employment wherein he was called. [3] And for their labor they may receive all necessary things, except money. And if they be in want, let them seek for alms like other brothers. And they may have the tools and implements necessary for their work. Let all the brothers apply themselves with diligence to good works, for it is written : " Be always busy in some good work, that the devil may find thee occupied ; " [4] and again : " Idleness is an enemy to the soul." [5] Therefore the servants of God ought always to continue in prayer or in some other good work.

Let the brothers take care that wherever they may be, whether in hermitages or in other places, they never appropriate any place to themselves, or maintain it against another. And whoever may come to them, either a friend or a foe, a thief or a robber, let them receive him kindly. And wherever the brothers are and in whatsoever place they may find themselves, let them spiritually and diligently show reverence

[1] Ps. 127 : 2.   [2] II Thess. 3 : 10.
[3] See I Cor. 7 : 24.
[4] St. Jerome says : "Semper facito aliquid boni operis, ut diabolus te inveniat occupatum." Epis. 125 (alias 4), n. 11.
[5] St. Anselm says : "Otiositas inimica est animae." Epist. 49.

and honor toward one another without murmuring.[1] And let them take care not to appea
exteriorly sad and gloomy like hypocrites, but
let them show themselves to be joyful an
contented in the Lord, merry and becomingly
courteous.[2]

8.—*That the Brothers must not receive Money.*

The Lord commands in the Gospel : "Take
heed, beware of all malice and avarice and guard
yourselves from the solicitudes of this world,
and the cares of this life."[3]   Therefore let none
of the brothers, wherever he may be or whither-
soever he may go, carry or receive money or coin
in any manner, or cause it to be received, either
for clothing, or for books, or as the price of
any labor, or indeed for any reason, except on
account of the manifest necessity of the sick
brothers.   For we ought not to have more use
and esteem of money and coin than of stones.
And the devil seeks to blind those who desire or
value it more than stones.   Let us therefore
take care lest after having left all things we lose
the kingdom of heaven for such a trifle.   And
if we should chance to find money in any place,
let us no more regard it than the dust we tread
under our feet,[4] for it is "vanity of vanities, and
all is vanity."[5]   And if perchance, which God

---

[1] See I Peter 4 : 9.   [2] See above, page 28,
[3] See Luke 12 : 15, and 21 : 34.
[4] See *Leg. III. Soc.*, n. 35.
[5] Eccle. 1 : 2.

forbid, it should happen that any brother should collect or have money or coin, except only because of the aforesaid necessity of the sick, let all the brothers hold him for a false brother, a thief, a robber, and one having a purse, unless he should become truly penitent. And let the brothers in nowise receive money for alms [1] or cause it to be received, seek it or cause it to be sought, or money for other houses or places; nor let them go with any person seeking money or coin for such places. But the brothers may perform all other services which are not contrary to our life, with the blessing of God. The brothers may however for the manifest necessity of the lepers ask alms for them. But let them be very wary of money. But let all the brothers likewise take great heed not to search the world for any filthy lucre.

9.—*Of asking for Alms.*

Let all the brothers strive to follow the humility and poverty of our Lord Jesus Christ, and let them remember that we ought to have nothing else in the whole world, except as the Apostle says: "Having food and wherewith to be covered, with these we are content.[2]" And they ought to rejoice when they converse with mean and despised persons, with the poor and

---

[1] O., Is. and Pis. read "money for alms;" Clar. and Spec. read "alms of money;" An., Mon. and Wadding read "money or alms."

[2] I Tim. 6: 8.

the weak, with the infirm and lepers, and with
those who beg in the streets. And when it may
be necessary, let them go for alms) And let
them not be ashamed thereof, but rather remember that our Lord Jesus Christ, the Son of the
Living and Omnipotent God, set His face "as
a hard rock,"[1] and was not ashamed, and was
poor, and a stranger, and lived on alms, He Himself and the Blessed Virgin and His disciples.
And when men may treat them with contempt,
and refuse to give them an alms, let them give
thanks for this to God, because for these shames
they shall receive great honor before the tribunal
of our Lord Jesus Christ. And let them know
that the injuries shall not be imputed to those
who suffer them, but to those who offer them.
And alms is an inheritance and a right which is
due to the poor, which our Lord Jesus Christ
purchased for us. And the brothers who labor
in seeking it will have a great recompense, and
they will procure and acquire a reward for those
who give ; for all that men leave in this world
shall perish, but for the charity and alms-deeds
they have done they will receive a reward from
God.

And let one make known clearly his wants to
another, in order that he may find and receive
what are necessary for him. And let everyone
love and nourish his brother as a mother loves
and nourishes her son, in so far as God gives
them grace. And "let not him that eateth des-

[1] Is. 50 : 7.

pise him that eateth not ; and he that eateth not, let him not judge him that eateth."[1] And whensoever a necessity shall arise, it is lawful for all the brothers, wherever they may be, to eat of all food that men can eat, as our Lord said of David, who "did eat the loaves of proposition, which was not lawful to eat but for the priests."[2] And let them remember what the Lord says : "and take heed to yourselves, lest perhaps your hearts be overcharged with surfeiting and drunkenness, and the cares of this life : and that they come upon you suddenly. For as a snare shall it come upon all that sit upon the face of the whole earth."[3] And in like manner in time of manifest necessity let all the brothers act in their needs, as our Lord shall give them grace, for necessity has no law.

10.—*Of the sick Brothers.*

If any of the brothers fall into sickness, wherever he may be, let the others not leave him, unless one of the brothers, or more if it be necessary, be appointed to serve him as they would wish to be served themselves ; but in urgent necessity they may commit him to some person who will take care of him in his infirmity. And I ask the sick brother that he give thanks to the Creator for all things, and that he desire to be as God wills him to be, whether sick or well ; for all whom the Lord has predestined to eternal

---

[1] Rom. 14: 3. [2] Mark 2: 26.
[3] Luke 21 : 34–35.

life[1] are disciplined by the rod of afflictions and infirmities, and the spirit of compunction ; as the Lord says : "Such as I love I rebuke and chastise."[2] If, however, he be disquieted and angry, either against God or against the brothers, or perhaps ask eagerly for remedies, desiring too much to deliver his body which is soon to die, which is an enemy to the soul, this comes to him from evil and he is fleshly, and seems not to be of the brothers, because he loves his body more than his soul.[3]

11.—That the Brothers ought not to speak evil or detract, but ought to love one another.

And let all the brothers take care not to calumniate anyone, nor to contend in words ;[4] let them indeed study to maintain silence as far as God gives them grace. Let them also not dispute among themselves or with others, but let them be ready to answer with humility, saying : "we are unprofitable servants."[5] And let them not be angry, for "whosoever is angry with his brother shall be in danger of the judgment. And whosoever shall say to his brother, *Raca*, shall be in danger of the council. And whosoever shall say, Thou fool, shall be in danger of hell fire."[6] And let them love one another, as the

[1] See Acts 13 : 48.   Apoc. 3 : 19.
[3] See 2 Cel. 3, 110; also Hugo le Digne, *l. c.*, fol. 68 v. and *Spec. Perf.* (ed. Sabatier), chap. 42.
[4] See II Tim. 2 : 14.   Luke 17 : 10.
[6] Matt. 5 : 22.

Lord says : " This is My commandment, that you love one another, as I have loved you.["] And let them show their love by the works [2] they do for each other, according as the Apostle says : " let us not love in word or in tongue, but in deed and in truth." [3] Let them " speak evil of no man,"[4] nor murmur, nor detract others, for it is written : " Whisperers and detractors are hateful to God."[5] And let them be " gentle, showing all mildness toward all men."[6] Let them not judge and not condemn, and, as the Lord says, let them not pay attention to the least sins of others, but rather let them recount their own in the bitterness of their soul. [7] And let them " strive to enter by the narrow gate,"[8] for the Lord says : " How narrow is the gate, and strait is the way that leadeth to life, and few there are that find it !" [9]

12.—*Of avoiding unbecoming Looks and the Company of Women.*

Let all the brothers, wherever they are or may go, carefully avoid unbecoming looks, and company of women, and let no one converse with them alone.[10] Let the priests speak to them honestly, giving them penance or some spiritual counsel.   And let no woman whatsoever be re-

---

[1] John 15 : 12.
[2] Jas. 2[2]: 18.
[3] I John 3 : 18.
[4] Tit. 3 : 2.
[5] Rom. 1 : 29-30.
[6] Tit. 3 : 2.
[7] Is. 38 : 15.
[8] Luke 13 : 24.
[9] Matt. 7 : 14.
[10] See above, p. 29.

ceived to obedience by any brother,[1] but spiritual counsel being given to her let her do penance where she wills. Let us all carefully watch over ourselves, and hold all our members in subjection, for the Lord says : " Whosoever shall look on a woman to lust after her, hath already committed adultery with her in his heart."[2]

13.—*Of the Punishment of Fornicators.*

If any brother by the instigation of the devil should commit fornication, let him be deprived of the habit of the Order which he has lost by his base iniquity and let him put it aside wholly, and let him be altogether expelled from our religion. And let him afterwards do penance for his sins.

14.—*How the Brothers should go through the World.*

When the brothers travel through the world, let them carry nothing by the way, neither bag, nor purse, nor bread, nor money, nor a staff. And whatsoever house they shall enter, let them first say, " Peace be to this house," and remaining in the same house, let them eat and drink what things they have.[3] Let them not resist evil,[4] but if anyone should strike them on the cheek, let them turn to him the other ; and if anyone take away their garment, let them not

[1] This prohibition refers to a vow of obedience made by a woman to her spiritual director, as Fr. Van Ortroy points out. See *Anal. Boll* , t. xxiv, fasc. iv, p. 523.

[2] Matt. 5: 28.   [3] See Luke 9 : 3 ; 10: 4–8.

[4] See Matt. 5: 39.

forbid him the tunic also. Let them give to everyone that asketh them, and if anyone take away their goods, let them not ask them again.[1]

15.—That the Brothers may not keep Beasts nor ride.

I enjoin all the brothers, both clerics and laics, that when they travel through the world, or reside in places, they in no wise, either with them or with others or in any other way, have any kind of beast of burden. Nor is it lawful for them to ride on horseback unless they are compelled by infirmity or great necessity.

16.—Of those who go among the Saracens and other Infidels.

The Lord says : " Behold, I send you as sheep in the midst of wolves. Be ye therefore wise as serpents and simple as doves."[2] Wherefore, whoever of the brothers may wish, by divine inspiration, to go among the Saracens and other infidels, let them go with the permission of their minister and servant. But let the minister give them leave and not refuse them, if he sees they are fit to be sent ; he will be held to render an account to the Lord if in this or in other things he acts indiscreetly. The brothers, however, who go may conduct themselves in two ways spiritually among them. One way is not to make disputes or contentions ; but let them be " sub-

---

[1] See Luke 6 : 29-30.　　　　[2] Matt. 10 : 16.

ject to every human creature for God's sake,"[1]
yet confessing themselves to be Christians. The
other way is that when they see it is pleasing to
God, they announce the Word of God, that they
may believe in Almighty God,—Father, and Son,
and Holy Ghost, the Creater of all, our Lord
the Redeemer and Saviour the Son, and that
they should be baptized and be made Christians,
because, "unless a man be born again of water
and the Holy Ghost, he cannot enter into the
kingdom of God." [2]

These and other things which please God they
may say to them, for the Lord says in the Gospel: "Everyone that shall confess Me before
men, I will also confess him before My Father
who is in heaven;"[3] and "he that shall be
ashamed of Me and My words, of him the Son
of Man shall be ashamed, when He shall come in
His majesty and that of His Father, and of the
holy angels." [4]

And let all the brothers, wherever they may
be, remember that they have given themselves,
and have relinquished their bodies to our Lord
Jesus Christ; and for love of Him they ought
to expose themselves to enemies both visible and
invisible, for the Lord says: "Whosoever shall
lose his life for My sake, shall save it "[5] in eternal
life. "Blessed are they that suffer persecution
for justice' sake, for theirs is the kingdom of

[1] I Pet. 2 : 13.   [2] John 3 : 5.
[3] Matt. 10 : 32.   [4] Luke 9 : 26.
[5] Mark 8 : 35; Luke 9 : 24.

heaven."[1] "If they have persecuted Me, they will also persecute you."[2] If however they should persecute you in one city, flee to another.[3] "Blessed are ye when they shall revile you, and persecute you, and speak all that is evil against you, untruly, for My sake."[4] "Be glad in that day and rejoice, for your reward is great in heaven."[5] "I say to you, my friends, be not afraid of them who kill the body, and after that have no more that they can do."[6] "See that ye are not troubled."[7] "In your patience you shall possess your souls."[8] "But he that shall persevere unto the end, he shall be saved."[9]

17.—*Of Preachers.*

Let none of the brothers preach contrary to the form and institution of the holy Roman Church, and unless this has been conceded to him by his minister. But let the minister take care that he does not grant this leave indiscreetly to anyone. Nevertheless, let all the brothers preach by their works. And let no minister or preacher appropriate to himself the ministry of brothers or the office of preaching, but let him give up his office without any contradiction at whatever hour it may be enjoined him. Wherefore I beseech in the charity which God is[10] all

[1] Matt. 5 : 10.
[2] John 15 : 20.
[3] See Matt. 10 : 23.
[4] Matt. 5 : 11–12.
[5] Luke 6 : 23.
[6] Luke 12 : 4.
[7] Matt. 24 : 6.
[8] Luke 21 : 19.
[9] Matt. 10 : 22.
[10] See I John 4 : 8.

my brothers, preachers, prayers, or laborers, both clerics and laics, that they study to humble themselves in all things and that they glory not, nor rejoice, nor inwardly exalt themselves on account of good words and works, nor indeed for any good which God may sometimes say or do and operate in them or by them, according to what the Lord says: "But yet rejoice not, in this that spirits are subject unto you."[1] And let us know for certain that nothing belongs to us but vices and sins. And we ought rather to rejoice when we "fall into divers temptations,"[2] and when we bear some afflictions or sorrows of soul or body in this world for the sake of eternal life. Let us then all, brothers, avoid all pride and vainglory. Let us keep ourselves from the wisdom of this world, and the prudence of the flesh; for the spirit of the world wishes and cares much for words, but little for work; and it seeks not religion and interior sanctity of spirit, but wishes and desires a religion and sanctity appearing from without to men. And these are they of whom the Lord says: "Amen, I say unto you, they have received their reward."[3] But the spirit of the Lord wishes the flesh to be mortified and despised, and to be considered vile, abject, and contemptible; and it studies humility and patience, pure simplicity, and true peace of mind, and always desires above all things divine fear and divine wisdom, and the divine love of the Father, and the Son, and the Holy Ghost.

[1] Luke 10: 20.   [2] James 1: 2.   [3] Matt. 6: 2.

And let us refer all good to the Lord God most High and Supreme ; let us acknowledge that all good belongs to Him, and let us give thanks for all to Him from whom all good proceeds. And may He, the most High and Supreme, only True God, have, and may there be rendered to Him and may He receive, all honors and reverences, all praises and benedictions, all thanks and all glory, to whom all good belongs, who alone is good.[1] And when we see or hear evil said or God blasphemed, let us bless and thank and praise the Lord who is blessed for ever. Amen.

18.—*How the Ministers should meet together.*

Each minister may assemble with his brothers every year wherever he may please on the Feast of St. Michael the Archangel, to treat of those things which belong to God. And let all the ministers who are in parts beyond the sea and beyond the mountains come once in three years, and the other ministers once every year to the chapter on Whit Sunday, at the Church of St. Mary of the Portiuncula, unless it be otherwise ordered by the minister and servant of the whole brotherhood.

19.—*That all the Brothers must live in a Catholic way.*

Let all the brothers be Catholics, and live and speak in a Catholic manner. But if anyone

[1] See Luke 18 : 19.

should err from the Catholic faith and life in word or in deed, and will not amend, let him be altogether expelled from our fraternity. And let us hold all clerics and religious as our masters in those things which regard the salvation of souls, if they do not deviate from our religion, and let us reverence their office and order and administration in the Lord.

20.—*Of the Confession of the Brothers and of the Reception of the Body and Blood of our Lord Jesus Christ.*

Let my blessed brothers, both clerics and laics, confess their sins to priests of our religion. And if they cannot do this, let them confess to other discreet and Catholic priests, knowing firmly and hoping that from whatever Catholic priests they may receive penance and absolution, they will undoubtedly be absolved from these sins if they take care to observe humbly and faithfully the penance enjoined them. If however they cannot then have a priest, let them confess to their brother, as the Apostle James says : " Confess your sins to one another ; " [1] but let them not on this account fail to have recourse to priests, for to priests alone the power of binding and loosing has been given. And thus contrite and having confessed, let them receive the Body and Blood of our Lord Jesus Christ with great humility and veneration, calling to mind

[1] James 5 : 16.

what the Lord Himself says : " He that eateth
My Flesh and drinketh My Blood hath everlasting life ; " [1] and " Do this for a commemoration
of Me." [2]

21.—*Of the Praise and Exhortation which all the Brothers may make.*

And this or the like exhortation and praise all
my brothers may announce with the blessing of
God, whenever it may please them among whatever men they may be : Fear and honor, praise
and bless God, give thanks [3] and adore the Lord
God Almighty in Trinity and Unity, Father, and
Son, and Holy Ghost, the Creator of all. " Do
penance," [4] brin forth fruits worthy of penance, [5]
for know that w must soon die. " Give and it
shall be given to you ; " [6] " Forgive, and you
shall be forgiven." [7] And if you do not forgive
men their sins, the Lord will not forgive you
your sins. [8] Confess all your sins. [9] Blessed are
they who shall die in penitence, for they shall
be in the kingdom of heaven. Woe to those
who do not die in penitence, for they shall be
the children of the devil, whose works they do, [10]
and they shall go into eternal fire. Beware and
abstain from all evil, and persevere in good
until the end.

[1] John 6 : 55.
[2] I Thess. 5 : 18.
[5] Luke 3 : 8.
[7] Luke 6 : 37.
[9] See James 5 : 16.

Luke 22 : 19.
Matt. 3 : 2.
Luke 6 : 38.
See Mark 11 : 26.
See John 8 : 44.

22.—*Of the Admonition of the Brothers.*

Let us all, brothers, give heed to what the Lord says : " Love your enemies, and do good to them that hate you."[1] For our Lord Jesus, whose footsteps we ought to follow,[2] called His betrayer friend,[3] and offered Himself willingly to His crucifiers. Therefore all those who unjustly inflict upon us tribulations and anguishes, shames and injuries, sorrows and torments, martyrdom and death, are our friends whom we ought to love much, because we gain eternal life by that which they make us suffer. And let us hate our body with its vices and sins, because by living carnally it wishes to deprive us of the love of our Lord Jesus Christ and eternal life, and to lose itself with all else in hell ; for we by our own fault are corrupt, miserable, and averse to good, but prompt and willing to evil ; because, as the Lord says in the Gospel : from the heart of men proceed and come evil thoughts, adulteries, fornications, murders, thefts, covetousness, wickedness, deceit, lasciviousness, an evil eye, false testimonies, blasphemy, foolishness.[4] All these evils come from within, from the heart of man, and these are what defile a man.

But now, after having renounced the world, we have nothing else to do but to be solicitous, to follow the will of God, and to please Him.

[1] Matt. 5 : 44. [2] See I Peter 2 : 21.
[3] See Matt. 26 : 50.
[4] See Matt. 15 : 19, and Mark 7 : 21-22.

Let us take much care that we be not the wayside, or the stony or thorny ground, according to what the Lord says in the Gospel : The seed is the word of God. And that which fell by the wayside and was trampled under foot are they that hear the word and do not understand ; then the devil cometh, and snatcheth that which has been sown in their hearts and taketh the word out of their hearts, lest believing they should be saved. But that which fell upon the rock are they who, when they hear the word, at once receive it with joy ; but when tribulation and persecution arise on account of the word, they are immediately scandalized, and these have no roots in themselves, but are for a while, for they believe for a while, and in time of temptation fall away. But that which fell among thorns are they who hear the word of God, and the solicitude and cares of this world, the fallacies of riches, and the desire of other things entering in choke the word, and it becomes unfruitful. But that sown on good ground are they who, in a good and best heart, hearing the word understand and keep it, and bring forth fruit in patience.[1]

And for this reason, brothers, let us, as the Lord says, "let the dead bury their dead." [2] And let us be much on our guard against the malice and cunning of Satan, who desires that man should not give his heart and mind to the

[1] See Matt. 13 : 19–23 ; Mark 4 : 15–20 ; Luke 8 : 11–15.
[2] Matt. 8 : 22.

Lord God, and who going about seeks to seduce
the heart of man under pretext of some reward
or benefit, to smother the words and precepts of
the Lord from memory, and who wishes to blind
the heart of man by wordly business and cares,
and to dwell there, as the Lord says : " When
an unclean spirit is gone out of a man, he walk-
eth through dry places seeking rest and findeth
none ; then he saith : 'I will return into my
house whence I came out.' And coming he
findeth it empty, swept, and garnished. Then
he goeth and taketh with him seven other spirits
more wicked than himself, and they enter in, and
dwell there ; and the last state of that man is
made worse than the first."[1] Wherefore let us
all, brothers, watch much, lest under pretext of
some reward or labor or aid we lose or separate
our mind and heart from the Lord. But I beseech
all the brothers, both the ministers and others,
in the charity which God is,[2] that, overcoming
all obstacles and putting aside all care and solicitude, they strive in the best manner they are
able, to serve, love, and honor the Lord God with
a clean heart and a pure mind, which He seeks
above all. And let us always make in us a tabernacle and dwelling-place for Him, who is the
Lord God Omnipotent, Father, and Son, and
Holy Ghost, who says : "Watch, therefore,
praying at all times, that you may be accounted
worthy to escape " all the evils " that are to come,

[1] Matt. 12 : 43-45 ; see Luke 11 : 24-26.
[2] See I John 4 : 16.

and to stand before the Son of Man."[1] And when you stand to pray,[2] say, "Our Father, who art in heaven." And let us adore Him with a pure heart, for "we ought always to pray, and not to faint,"[3] for the Father seeks such adorers. "God is a Spirit, and they that adore Him, must adore Him in spirit and in truth."[4] And let us have recourse to Him as the "Shepherd and Bishop of our souls,"[5] who says: "I am the Good Shepherd," who feed My sheep, "and I lay down My life for My flock."[6] But all you are brothers. "And call none your father upon earth; for one is your Father who is in heaven. Neither be ye called masters, for one is your master, who is in heaven, Christ."[7] "If you abide in Me, and My words abide in you, you shall ask whatever you will, and it shall be done unto you."[8] "Where there are two or three gathered together in My Name, there am I in the midst of them."[9] "Behold, I am with you all days, even to the consummation of the world."[10] "The words that I have spoken to you are spirit and life."[11] "I am the Way, the Truth, and the Life."[12]

Let us therefore hold fast the words, the life and doctrine and holy Gospel of Him who deigned for us to ask His Father to manifest to

---

[1] Luke 21 : 36.
[2] See Mark 11 : 25.
[3] Luke 18 : 1.
[4] John 4 : 24.
[5] I Peter 2 : 25.
See John 10 : 11 and 15.
[7] See Matt. 23 : 8–10.
[8] John 15 : 7.
[9] Matt. 18 : 20.
[10] Matt. 28 : 20.
John 6 : 64.
John 14 : 6.

us His Name, saying : Father, I have manifested
Thy Name to the men whom Thou hast given
Me because the words which Thou gavest Me I
have given to them, and they have received them,
and have known in very deed that I came forth
out of Thee, and they have believed that Thou
didst send Me. I pray for them, I pray not for
the world, but for them whom Thou hast given
Me, because they are Thine and all My things
are Thine. Holy Father, keep them in Thy
Name whom Thou hast given Me, that they may
be one, as We also are. These things I speak in
the world that they may have joy filled in themselves. I have given them Thy word, and the
world hath hated them, because they are not of
the world, as I also am not of the world. I pray
not that Thou shouldst take them out of the
world, but that Thou shouldst keep them from
evil. Sanctify them in truth. Thy word is truth.
As Thou hast sent Me into the world, I have sent
them into the world. And for them I do sanctify
Myself, that they may be sanctified in truth.
Not for them only do I pray, but for them also
who through their word shall believe in Me,
that they may be consummated in one, and that
the world may know that Thou hast sent Me,
and hast loved them, as Thou hast also loved
Me. And I have made known Thy Name to
them, that the love wherewith Thou hast loved
Me may be in them, and I in them. Father, I
will that where I am, they also whom Thou hast

given Me may be with Me, that they may see Thy glory in Thy kingdom.[1]

23.—*Prayer, Praise, and Thanksgiving.*[2]

Almighty, most Holy, most High and Supreme God, Holy and Just Father, Lord King of heaven and earth, for Thyself we give thanks to Thee because by Thy holy will, and by Thine only Son, Thou hast created all things spiritual and corporal in the Holy Ghost and didst place us made to Thine image and likeness[3] in paradise, whence we fell by our own fault. And we give Thee thanks because, as by Thy Son Thou didst create us, so by the true and holy love with which Thou hast loved us,[4] Thou didst cause Him, true God and true Man, to be born of the glorious and ever-Virgin, most Blessed holy Mary, and didst will that He should redeem us captives by His Cross and Blood and Death. And we give thanks to Thee because Thy Son Himself is to come again in the glory of His Majesty to put the wicked who have not done penance for their sins, and have not known Thee, in eternal fire, and to say to all who have known Thee and adored Thee, and served Thee in penance: "Come, ye blessed of My Father, possess the kingdom prepared for you from the beginning of the world."[5]

---

[1] See John 17: 6–26.
[2] The *Speculum Minorum* condenses this chapter.
[3] See Gen. 1 : 26 ; 2: 15.
[4] See John 17: 26.   [5] Matt. 25: 34.

And since all we wretches and sinners are not worthy to name Thee, we humbly beseech Thee, that our Lord Jesus Christ, Thy beloved Son, in whom Thou art well pleased,[1] together with the Holy Ghost, the Paraclete, may give thanks to Thee as it is pleasing to Thee and Them, for all ; He suffices Thee always for all through whom Thou hast done so much for us. Alleluia. And we earnestly beg the glorious Mother, the most Blessed Mary ever-Virgin, Blessed Michael, Gabriel, Raphael, and all the choirs of the blessed spirits, seraphim, cherubim, and thrones, dominations, principalities and powers, virtues, angels and archangels, blessed John the Baptist, John the Evangelist, Peter, Paul, the blessed patriarchs and prophets, innocents, apostles, evangelists, disciples, martyrs, confessors, virgins, blessed Elias and Enoch, and all the Saints who have been and are, and shall be, for Thy love, that they may, as it is pleasing to Thee, give thanks for these things to the most high, true God, eternal and living, with Thy most dear Son, our Lord Jesus Christ, and the Holy Ghost, the Paraclete, for ever and ever. Amen. Alleluia.

And all we, brothers minor, useless servants, humbly entreat and beseech all those within the holy Catholic and Apostolic Church wishing to serve God, and all ecclesiastical Orders, priests, deacons, subdeacons, acolytes, exorcists, lectors, door-keepers, and all clerics ; all religious men

[1] See Matt. 17 : 5.

and women, all boys and children, poor and needy, kings and princes, laborers, husbandmen, servants and masters, all virgins, continent, and married people, laics, men and women, all infants, youths, young men and old, healthy and sick, all small and great, and all peoples, clans, tribes, and tongues, all nations and all men in all the earth, who are and shall be, that we may persevere in the true faith and in doing penance, for otherwise no one can be saved. Let us all love with all our heart, with all our soul, with all our mind, with all our strength and fortitude, with all our understanding and with all our powers,[1] with our whole might and whole affection, with our innermost parts, our whole desires, and wills, the Lord God, who has given, and gives to us all, the whole body, the whole soul, and our life; who has created and redeemed us, and by His mercy alone will save us; who has done and does all good to us, miserable and wretched, vile, unclean, ungrateful, and evil.

Let us therefore desire nothing else, wish for nothing else, and let nothing please and delight us except our Creator and Redeemer, and Saviour, the only true God, who is full of good, all good, entire good, the true and supreme good, who alone is good,[2] merciful and kind, gentle and sweet, who alone is holy, just, true, and upright, who alone is benign, pure, and clean, from whom, and through whom, and in whom is all mercy,

[1] See Deut. 6: 5; Mark 12: 30 and 33; Luke 10: 27.
[2] See Luke 18: 19.

all grace, all glory of all penitents and of the just, and of all the blessed rejoicing in heaven. Let nothing therefore hinder us, let nothing separate us, let nothing come between us. Let us all, everywhere, in every place, at every hour, and at all times, daily and continually believe, truly and humbly, and let us hold in our hearts, and love, honor, adore, serve, praise and bless, glorify and exalt, magnify and give thanks to the most High and Supreme, Eternal God, in Trinity and Unity, to the Father, and Son, and Holy Ghost, to the Creator of all, to the Saviour of all who believe and hope in Him, and love Him, who, without beginning or end, is inmutable, invisible, unerring, ineffable, incomprehensible, unfathomable, blessed, praiseworthy, glorious, exalted, sublime, most high, sweet, amiable, lovable, and always wholly desirable above all forever and ever.

In the Name of the Lord, I beseech all the brothers that they learn the tenor and sense of those things that are written in this life for the salvation of our souls, and frequently recall them to mind. And I pray God that He who is Almighty, Three in One, may bless all who teach, learn, hold, remember, and fulfil those things as often as they repeat and do what is there written for our salvation. And I entreat all, kissing their feet, to love greatly, keep and treasure up these things. And on the part of Almighty God and of the Lord Pope, and by obedience, I, Brother Francis, strictly command and enjoin that no one subtract from those things that are written in this life, or add anything written to it over and above, and that the brothers have no other Rule.

Glory be to the Father, and to the Son, and to the Holy Ghost. As it was in the beginning, is now and ever shall be, world without end. Amen.

SECOND RULE OF THE FRIARS MINOR.[1]

1.—*In the Name of the Lord begins the life of the Minor Brothers.*

The Rule and life of the Minor Brothers is this, namely, to observe the holy Gospel of our Lord Jesus Christ, by living in obedience, without property and in chastity. Brother Francis promises obedience and reverence to the Lord Pope Honorius and to his successors canonically elected and to the Roman Church. And let the other brothers be bound to obey Brother Francis and his successors.

2.—*Of those who wish to embrace this Life and how they ought to be received.*

If any wish to embrace this life and come to our brothers, let them send them to their pro-

---

[1] This is the text of 1223 and represents the Rule at present observed throughout the first Franciscan Order. It is here translated according to the text of the original Bull which is preserved at the Sacro Convento in Assisi. A duplicate of this document, contained in the Pontifical Register at the Vatican Library, has been consulted for certain passages less legible in the original.

vincial ministers, to whom alone and not to others is accorded the power of receiving brothers. But let the ministers diligently examine them regarding the Catholic faith and the Sacraments of the Church. And if they believe all these things, and if they will confess them faithfully and observe them firmly to the end, and if they have no wives, or, if they have and their wives have already entered a monastery, or have, with the authority of the diocesan bishop, given them permission after having made a vow of continence, and if the wives be of such an age that no suspicion may arise concerning them, let them [the ministers] say to them the word of the holy Gospel,[1] that they go and sell all their goods and strive to distribute them to the poor. If they should not be able to do this, their good will suffices. And the brothers and their ministers must take care not to be solicitous about their temporal affairs, that they may freely do with their affairs whatsoever the Lord may inspire them. If, however, counsel should be required, the ministers shall have power of sending them to some God-fearing men by whose advice their goods may be distributed to the poor. Afterwards, let them give them clothes of probation, to wit, two tunics without a hood and a cord and breeches and a chaperon reaching to the cord, unless at some time the same ministers may decide otherwise according to God. The year of probation being finished, they shall be received

[1] See Matt. 19 : 21.

to obedience, promising to observe always this life and rule. And according to the command of the Lord Pope[1] in no wise shall it be allowed them to go out of this religion, because, according to the holy Gospel : "No man putting his hand to the plough and looking back is fit for the kingdom of God."[2] And let those who have already promised obedience have one tunic with a hood, and if they wish it another without a hood. And those who are obliged by necessity may wear shoes. And let all the brothers be clothed in poor garments and they may patch them with pieces of sackcloth and other things, with the blessing of God. I admonish and exhort them not to despise or judge men whom they see clothed in fine and showy garments using dainty meats and drinks, but rather let each one judge and despise himself.

3.—*Of the Divine Office, and of Fasting; and how the Brothers must go through the world.*

Let the clerics perform the Divine Office according to the order of the holy Roman Church, with the exception of the Psalter ; wherefore they may have breviaries.[3] But let the laics say twenty-four *Paternosters* for Matins ; five for

---

[1] See above, page 34, note 2.   [2] Luke 9 : 62.

[3] This passage : *ex quo habere poterunt breviaria*, may also be rendered : "as soon as they can have breviaries." (See Wadding, *Opusc.*, p. 179.) But the latter translation has less foundation.

Lauds ; for Prime, Tierce, Sext and Nones,—for each of these, seven ; for Vespers, however, twelve, for Compline seven ; and let them pray for the dead.

And let them fast from the feast of All Saints until the Nativity of the Lord. But the holy Lent which begins from Epiphany and continues for forty days, which the Lord has consecrated by His holy fast,[1]—may those who keep it voluntarily be blessed by the Lord and those who do not wish may not be constrained. But they must fast during the other one until the Resurrection of the Lord. At other times, however, they shall not be obliged to fast, except on Fridays. But in time of manifest necessity the brothers shall not be bound to corporal fasting.

I indeed counsel, warn, and exhort my brothers in the Lord Jesus Christ that when they go through the world they be not litigious nor contend in words,[2] nor judge others ; but that they be gentle, peaceful, and modest, meek and humble, speaking honestly to all as is fitting. And they must not ride on horseback unless compelled by manifest necessity or infirmity. Into whatsoever house they may enter let them first say : Peace be to this house ! And, according to the holy Gospel, it is lawful to eat of all foods which are set before them.[3]

[1] See Matt. 4 : 2.
[2] See Tit. 3 : 2 and II Tim. 2 : 14.
[3] See Luke 10 : 5 and 8.

4.—*That the Brothers must not receive money.*

I strictly enjoin on all the brothers that in no wise they receive coins or money, either themselves or through an interposed person. Nevertheless, for the necessities of the sick and for clothing the other brothers, let the ministers and custodes alone take watchful care through spiritual friends, according to places and times and cold climates, as they shall see expedient in the necessity, saving always that, as has been said, they shall not receive coins or money.

5.—*Of the manner of working.*

Let those brothers to whom the Lord has given the grace of working labor faithfully and devoutly, so that in banishing idleness, the enemy of the soul, they do not extinguish the spirit of holy prayer and devotion, to which all temporal things must be subservient. They may, however, receive as the reward of their labor, the things needful for the body for themselves and their brothers, with the exception of coins or money, and that humbly, as befits the servants of God and the followers of most holy poverty

6.—*That the Brothers shall appropriate nothing to themselves: and of seeking Alms and of the Sick Brothers.*

The brothers shall appropriate nothing to themselves, neither a house nor place nor anything.   And as pilgrims and strangers[1] in this world, serving the Lord in poverty and humility, let them go confidently in quest of alms, nor ought they to be ashamed, because the Lord made Himself poor for us in this world.   This, my dearest brothers, is the height of the most sublime poverty which has made you heirs and kings of the kingdom of heaven : poor in goods, but exalted in virtue.   Let that be your portion, for it leads to the land of the living ; [2] cleaving to it unreservedly, my best beloved brothers, for the Name of our Lord Jesus Christ, never desire to possess anything else under heaven.

And wheresoever the brothers are and may find themselves, let them mutually show among themselves that they are of one household. And let one make known his needs with confidence to the other, for, if a mother nourishes and loves her carnal son, how much more earnestly ought one to love and nourish his spiritual brother ! And if any of them should fall into illness, the other brothers must serve him as they would wish to be served themselves.

7.—*Of the Penance to be imposed on Brothers who sin.*

If any of the brothers, at the instigation of the enemy, sin mortally by those sins for which it has been ordained among the brothers that

[1] See I Peter 2 : 11.
[2] See Ps. 141 : 6. It was this Psalm that St. Francis recited at the hour of death.

recourse should be had to the provincial ministers alone, the aforesaid brothers are bound to have recourse to them as soon as possible, without delay. But let the ministers themselves, if they are priests, impose penance on them with mercy ; if however they are not priests, let them have it imposed by other priests of the Order, as it may seem to them most expedient, according to God. And they must beware lest they be angry or troubled on account of the sins of others, because anger and trouble impede charity in themselves and in others.

8.—*Of the Election of the Minister General of this Brotherhood, and of the Whitsun Chapter.*

All the brothers are bound always to have one of the brothers of this religion as minister general and servant of the whole brotherhood, and they are strictly bound to obey him. At his death the election of a successor must be made by the provincial ministers and custodes in the Whitsun Chapter, in which the provincial ministers are always bound to convene at the same time, whcresoever it may be appointed by the minister general, and that once in three years or at a longer or shorter interval as may be ordained by the said minister. And if at any time it should be apparent to the whole of the provincial ministers that the aforesaid minister general is not sufficient for the service and the common welfare of the brothers, let the aforesaid ministers, to whom the election has been committed, be bound to elect for themselves another as custos in the name of the Lord. But after the Whitsun Chapter the ministers and custodes may each, if they wish and it seem expedient to them, convoke their brothers to a chapter in their custodies once in the same year.

9.—*Of Preachers.*

The brothers must not preach in the diocese of any bishop when their doing so may be opposed by him. And let no one of the brothers dare to preach in any way to the people, unless he has been examined and approved by the minister general of this brotherhood, and the office of preaching conceded to him by the latter. I also warn and exhort the same brothers that in the preaching they do their words be fire-tried and pure [1] for the utility and edification of the people, announcing to them vices and virtues, punishment and glory, with brevity of speech because the Lord made His word short upon earth. [2]

10.—*Of the Admonition and Correction of the Brothers.*

Those brothers who are ministers and servants of the other brothers, shall visit and admonish their brothers, and shall humbly and charitably correct them, not commanding them

[1] See Ps. 11 : 7 and 17 : 31.   [2] See Rom. 9 : 28.

anything against their souls and our Rule. The brothers however who are subject must remember that, for God, they have renounced their own will. Wherefore I order them strictly to obey their ministers in all things which they have promised the Lord to observe and are not against their souls and our Rule. And wheresoever there are brothers who see and know that they are not able to observe the rule spiritually, they ought to and can recur to their ministers. And let the ministers receive them charitably and kindly and show so great familiarity toward them that they [the culprits] may speak and act with them as masters with their servants, for thus it ought to be, since the ministers are the servants of all the brothers.

. I also warn and exhort the brothers in the Lord Jesus Christ that they beware of all pride, vainglory, envy, covetousness,[1] the cares and solicitudes of this world, of detraction and murmuring. Let not those w o are ignorant of letters care to learn letters, b t let them con- si   ,   n a , t ey should desire to possess the spirit of the Lord and His holy operation, to pray always to Him with a pure heart and to have humility, patience in persecution and in infirmity and to love those who persecute, reprove, and accuse us, because the Lord has said: "Love your enemies . . . and pray for them that persecute and calumniate you."[2]   "Blessed are they that suffer perse-

[1] See Luke 12: 15.   [2] Matt. 5: 44.

cution for justice' sake, for theirs is the kingdom of heaven." [1] " But he that shall persevere to the end, he shall be saved." [2]

11.—*That the Brothers must not enter the Monas-
teries of Nuns.*

I strictly command all the brothers not to
have suspicious intimacy, or conferences with
women, and let none enter the monasteries of
nuns except those to whom special permission
has been granted by the Apostolic See.   And
let them not be godfathers of men or women,
that [3] scandal may not arise on this account
among the brothers or concerning the brothers.

12.—*Of those who go among the Saracens and
other Infidels.*

Let all of the brothers who by divine inspiration desire to go amongst the Saracens or other
infidels, ask leave therefor from their provincial
ministers.   But the ministers must give permission to go to none except to those whom they
see are fitted to be sent.

Moreover, I enjoin on the ministers, by obedience, that they ask of the Lord Pope one of the
Cardinals of the holy Roman Church to be
governor, protector, and corrector of this

---

[1] Matt. 5 : 10.   [2] Matt. 10 : 22.
[3] This is comformable to the original bull, which reads *nec
hac occasione;* but most of the printed texts give *ne,* "lest
scandal arise," instead of *nec.*

brotherhood, so that being always subject and submissive at the feet of the same holy Church, grounded in the Catholic faith,[1] we may observe poverty and humility and the holy Gospel of our Lord Jesus Christ, which we have firmly promised.

[1] See Col. 1 : 23.

V.

FRAGMENTS FROM THE RULE OF THE SISTERS OF
ST. CLARE.

Of the "many writings"[1] left by St. Francis to the
Poor Ladies at St. Damian's, only two fragments
are known to exist, and these have been preserved to
us through St. Clare herself, in so far as she incorporated them in the sixth chapter of her Rule. We have
it on the authority of Pope Gregory IX that St. Francis
wrote for St. Clare and her first companions a *formula
vitae*, or "little rule,".at the beginning of their religious life.[2]   But it was this same Pope Gregory IX,
then known as Cardinal Ugolino, who about 1219
composed a Rule for the Poor Ladies, which was accepted by St. Francis and confirmed by Honorius III.[3]
This Rule, as the Pontiff himself declares, was
solemnly professed by Clare and her Sisters and observed by them for many years in a praiseworthy
manner.[4]   Pope Innocent IV bears witness to the
same effect.   Writing to Blessed Agnes, Princess of
Bohemia (who had founded a house of the Second
Order at Prague), of this Rule, written by Cardinal

[1] "Plura scripta tradidit nobis," *Test. B Clarae.* See
Seraphicae Legislationis textus originales, p. 276.

[2] "When Clare," he says, "and some other devout women
in the Lord chose to serve under the same observance of religion, Blessed Francis gave them a little rule of life" (*formu-
lam vitae tradidit*).   See the bull *Angelis gaudium* of May 11,
1238 (*Bullar. Franc.*, t. I, p. 242).

[3] See *Bullar.*, I, 11 and 13: the letters *Prudentibus Virgini-
bus: Ann. Min.* I, 312: Gubernatis, *Orb. Seraph.* II, 603: also
Bullar. I, 4, n. (a).   The Rule may be found in the bull *Cum
omnis vera* of Gregory IX, of May 24, 1239. See *Bullar.*, t.
I, p. 263.

[4] See *Bullar.*, t. I, p. 242.

Ugolino, he says : "The Sisters of the Monastery of St. Damian and all others of your Order have laudably observed it from the time of its profession *until now.*"[1] These words were written on November 13, 1243.

In view of such testimony it is obviously a mistake to assert, as Wadding and some other writers do, that St. Clare abandoned this Rule in 1224, and professed another one written by St. Francis. It is also erroneous to suppose that St. Francis ever wrote a Rule for the Poor Ladies.[2] The one written about 1219, by Cardinal Ugolino, was recast by St. Clare herself toward the close of her life, and made to conform as far as possible to the Second Rule written by St. Francis for the Friars Minor. The Rule of the Poor Ladies, thus recast by St. Clare in a new form, was confirmed by Innocent IV, August 9, 1253, just two days before the death of the holy abbess.[3]

In the sixth chapter of this Rule, St. Clare describes the circumstances under which the two fragments of St. Francis' writings here given were composed. "After the Most High Heavenly Father deigned by His grace to enlighten my heart," St. Clare tells us, "to do penance after the example and teaching of our most blessed father, St. Francis, a little while after his own conversion, I, together with

---

[1] See *Bullar.*, t. I, p. 315.

[2] On the origin of the Second Order and the early Rule, see Lemmens: "Die Anfänge des Clarissenordens" in the *Römische Quartalschrift*, t. XVI, 1902, pp. 93-124, which is in the nature of a rejoinder to Dr. Lempp's article with the same title, published in Brieger's *Zeitschrift für Kirchengeschichte*, XIII, 181-245.

[3] This Rule is contained in the bull *Solet annuere*, of Innocent IV. See *Seraphicae Legislationis textus originales*, page 49 seq. See also *Bullar.*, I, 167; *Ann. Min.*, III, 287.

my sisters, voluntarily promised him obedience. But, seeing that we feared no poverty, toil, sorrow, abasement and contempt of the world, nay rather that we held them in great delight, the blessed father, moved by compassion, wrote us a rule of life[1] in this form " Then follows the first of the two fragments given below. Further on in the same chapter of her Rule, the holy abbess adds : "To the end that we and also those who might come after us should never fall away from the most holy poverty which we had undertaken, he again wrote to us shortly before his death[2] his last wish, saying ."[3] Then follows the second of the two fragments here given.

Both these pieces, which Wadding took for letters[4] addressed to St. Clare, are here translated according to the text of the Rule contained in the original bull of Innocent IV.[5] They are as follows :

1. FORM OF LIFE WHICH ST. FRANCIS WROTE FOR ST. CLARE.[6]

Since, by divine inspiration, you have made yourselves daughters and handmaids of the Most

[1] *Forma vivendi.* See *Seraph. Legislat.*, p. 62.

[2] The biographers place the writing of this fragment in the autumn of 1220, after St. Francis returned from the East.

[3] See *Seraph. Legislat.*, p. 63.

[4] They are numbered *IV* and *V* among the *Epistolae* in his edition of the *Opuscula*.

[5] This bull, which had been lost for several centuries, was brought to light early in 1893, after a protracted search in different countries; it was found wrapped within an old mantle of Saint Clare, preserved in the Monastery of Santa Chiara, at Assisi. See *Seraph. Legislat.*, pp. 2, seq. See also G. Cozza-Luzi : *Un autografo di Innocenzo IV e Memorie di S. Chiara*, ed. 2da., Rome, 1895.

[6] Some critics regard this fragment as a promise or engagement accompanying the *formula vitae* or as the beginning of

High Sovereign King, the Heavenly Father, and have espoused yourselves to the Holy Ghost, choosing to live according to the perfection of the holy Gospel, I will, and I promise to have always, by myself and my brothers, a diligent care and special solicitude for you, as for them. [1]

2. LAST WISH WHICH ST. FRANCIS WROTE TO ST. CLÁRE.

I, little brother Francis, wish to follow the life and poverty of Jesus Christ our Most High Lord and of His Most Holy Mother and to persevere therein until the end. And I beseech you all, my ladies, and counsel you, to live always in this most holy life and poverty. And watch yourselves well that you in no wise depart from it through the teaching or advice of any one.

the *formula* itself, and believe that the text of the latter, now lost, was also inserted originally in the sixth chapter of St. Clare's Rule. Be this as it may, it is certain that this chapter has been completely changed in several editions. In the vernacular versions of it, based on Wadding, the two fragments here given do not appear at all. See Fr. Van Ortroy, S.J., in *Anal. Boll.*, t. xxiv, fasc. iii, p. 412.

[1] See 2 Cel. 3, 132.

VI.

Testament of the Holy Father St. Francis.

The opuscule which St. Francis called his Testament is a precious document of the highest authority. Renan forsooth denied its authenticity, but rashly, for, as M. Sabatier rightly remarks,[1] this is not to be questioned.[2] The Testament corresponds throughout with the other writings of St. Francis, and moreover reveals his character and spirit in every line. But we are not reduced to internal proofs for its genuinity. All the historians, including Thomas of Celano,[3] and St. Bonaventure,[4] mention it,[5] while Gregory IX cites it textually in his bull *Quo elongati* of September 28, 1230. We know from this bull that the Saint's Testament was published a few days only before his death.[6] Everything seems to point to its having been written at the hermitage of the Celle near Cortona, during St. Francis' last visit there (summer of 1226), though some think it was dictated to Angelo Tancredi, one of the Three Companions, in the little hut nearest the Portiuncula which served as an infirmary and in which St. Francis died.

According to M. Sabatier, St. Francis wrote more than one testament. Indeed, the French critic goes so far as to say that at the end of each of his crises the Saint made his will anew,[7] and in support of this assertion cites Chapter 87 of his own edition of the

---

[1] Sabatier : *Vie de S. François ; Étude des Sources.*

[2] See also Goetz, *l. c.*, t. XXII, pp. 372 seq.

[3] See 1 Cel. 17; 2 Cel. 3, 99.   [4] See Bonav., *Leg. Maj.*, III, 2.

[5] It is also expressly cited in the *Leg. III Soc.* 11 and 29.

[6] "Circa ultimum vitae suae," etc. See *Bullarium Franc.*, t. I, p. 68.

[7] "À la fin de chacune de ces crises, il faisait de nouveau

Speculum Perfectionis, in which we read that during an illness (seemingly in April, 1226), St. Francis caused Brother Benedict of Prato to write down a blessing and some words of advice "in token of memory and benediction and testament." But surely from this narration we may not deduce the general proposition that St. Francis wrote "several testaments." The early Legends are silent except as to the one Testament here given, and all the passages which different writers quote " from the Testament " may be found in this one,—if we except two passages in M. Sabatier's edition of the *Speculum Perfectionis*. But it is not difficult to see that in both these places the *Speculum* is in error. In the ninth chapter it repeats incorrectly what Brother Leo elsewhere[1] relates, and in the fifty-fifth chapter the compiler of the *Speculum* is still more astray, as a comparison of this chapter with chapter twenty-seventh of Father Lemmens' edition of the *Speculum* clearly indicates. Both editions of the *Speculum* tell in almost the same words of St. Francis' love for the Church of the Portiuncula. M. Sabatier's edition says : "At his death he caused it to be written in the Testament that all the brothers should do likewise ;" whereas Father Lemmens' edition reads as follows : " Toward his death he bequeathed this Church to the brothers as a testament."[2]

The Testament is to be found among St. Francis' works in twelve of the codices above described,[3] to

son testament." *Speculum Perf.* (ed. Sabatier), p. **xxxiii**, note 2. See also *Speculum* (ed. Lemmens), No. 30.

[1] See *S. Francisci Intentio regulae*, nn. 14 and 15, in the *Documenta Antiqua Franciscana*, P. I, p. 97.

[2] See *Documenta Antiqua Franciscana*, P. II, p. 60.

[3] See page 3.

wit, those at Assisi,[1] Berlin, Florence (Ognissanti MSS.), St. Floriano, Liegnitz, Paris (Nat. lib. and Mazarin MSS. 989), Prague and Rome (St. Antony's and both Vatican MSS.), as well as in a fifteenth century MS. at the Hague (Municip. lib. cod. K. 54, fol. 3 v). The text here translated is that of the Assisi codex collated with those of Ognissanti, Florence, and St. Antony's, Rome, and with the versions of the Testament contained in the *Monumenta* (fol. 274 v) and *Firmamenta*[2] (fol. 16 v). Here begins the :

TESTAMENT OF THE HOLY FATHER ST. FRANCIS.

The Lord gave to me, Brother Francis, thus to begin to do penance ; for when I was in sin it seemed to me very bitter to see lepers, and the Lord Himself led me amongst them and I showed mercy to them.[3] And when I left them, that which had seemed to me bitter was changed for me into sweetness of body and soul. And afterwards I remained a little and I left the world. And the Lord gave me so much[4] faith

[1] The text of the Testament given by M. Sabatier in his edition of the *Speculum Perf.* is that of this Assisi MS.

[2] It may also be found in the *Speculum Minorum* (Tract. III, 8 r) and in the *Annales* of Wadding (ad an. 1226, 35).

[3] See 1 Cel. 17, where this passage of the Testament is quoted. See also Bonav. *Leg. Maj.*, II, 6 ; and *Leg. III Soc.* 11. Some texts instead of "*feci misericordiam cum illis*" give "*feci moram cum illis*" : "I made a sojourn with them." See *Miscell. Franc.*, III (1888), p. 70. It is interesting to note here how St Francis on the eve of his death, casting a backward glance over the ways by which he had been led, dwells on this incident which had marked a new era in his life.

[4] Cod. As. reads "*talem fidem*," "such faith."

in churches that I would simply pray and say thus : "We adore Thee Lord Jesus Christ here [1] and in all Thy churches which are in the whole world, and we bless Thee because by Thy holy cross Thou hast redeemed the world."

After that the Lord gave me, and gives me, so much faith in priests who live according to the form of the holy Roman Church, on account of their order,[2] that if they should persecute me, I would have recourse to them. And if I had as much wisdom as Solomon had, and if I should find poor priests of this world,[3] I would not preach against their will in the parishes in which they live. And I desire to fear, love, and honor them and all others as my masters ; and I do not wish to consider sin in them, for in them I sée the Son of God and they are my masters. And I do this because in this world, I see nothing corporally of the most high Son of God Himself except His most holy Body and Blood, which they receive and they alone administer to others. And I will that these most holy mysteries be honored and revered above all things and that they be placed in precious places. Wheresoever I find His most holy Names and written words in unseemly places, I wish to collect them, and I ask that they may be collected and put in a becoming place. And we

---

[1] Cod. As. and O. omit "here." (See 1 Cel. 45 ; and Bonav. *Leg. Maj.* 43, where this prayer may be found.) Cod. An. *Firm.* and Wadd. insert "here."

[2] Order, *i. e.*, sacerdotal character.

[3] Priests of the world, *i. e.*, secular priests.

ought to honor and venerate all theologians and those who minister to us the most holy Divine Words as those who minister to us spirit and life.[1]

And when the Lord gave me some brothers, no one showed me what I ought to do, but the Most High Himself revealed to me that I should live according to the form of the holy Gospel.[2] And I caused it to be written in few words and simply, and the Lord Pope confirmed it for me. And those who came to take this life upon themselves gave to the poor all that they might have and they[3] were content with one tunic, patched within and without, by those who wished,[4] with a cord and breeches, and we wished for no more.

We clerics said the Office like other clerics; the laics said the *Paternoster*, and we remained in the churches[5] willingly enough. And we were simple and subject to all. And I worked with my hands and I wish to work and I wish firmly that all the other brothers should work at some labor which is compatible with honesty. Let those who know not [how to work] learn, not through desire to receive the price of labor but for the sake of example and to repel idleness. And when the price of labor is not given to us,

[1] See 2 Cel. 3, 99, where this passage of the Testament is quoted; see also Bonav. *Epis. de tribus quaestionibus* in which it is also referred to. (*Opera Omnia*, t. VIII, p. 335.)

[2] See *Leg. III Soc.* 29, for reference to this passage.

[3] Cod. O. reads: *eramus* "we were content."

[4] Cod. As. omits *qui volebant*, "by those who wished."

[5] *Firm.* and Wadd. add: "poor and neglected churches."

let us have recourse to the table of the Lord, begging alms from door to door.

The Lord revealed to me this salutation, that we should say: "The Lord give thee peace."[1] Let the brothers take care not to receive on any account churches, poor dwelling-places, and all other things[2] that are constructed for them, unless they are as is becoming the holy poverty which we have promised in the Rule, always dwelling there as strangers and pilgrims.[3]

I strictly enjoin by obedience[4] on all the brothers that, wherever they may be, they should not dare, either themselves or by means of some interposed person,[5] to ask any letter in the Roman curia either for a church[6] or for any other place, nor under pretext of preaching, nor on account of their bodily persecution; but, wherever they are not received let them flee to another land to do penance, with the blessing of God. And I wish to obey the minister general of this brotherhood strictly and the guardian whom it may please him to give me. And I wish to be so captive in his hands that I cannot go or act beyond his obedience and his will because he is my master. And although I

[1] See Bonav. *Leg. Maj.*, III, 2.

[2] Cod. As. omits "other things," and O. omits "all other things."

[3] See *Documenta antiqua Franciscana*, P. I, page 98, n. 15, where this passage is cited among the *Verba quae scripsit Frater Leo*.

[4] Cod. O. omits "by obedience."

[5] Cod. An. omits this clause.

[6] Cod. O. omits "either for a church."

am simple and infirm, I desire withal always to have a cleric who will perform the office with me as it is contained in the Rule.

And let all the other brothers be bound to obey their guardian and to perform the office according to the Rule. And those who may be found not performing the office according to the Rule and wishing to change it in some way, or who are not Catholics, let all the brothers wherever they may be, if they find one of these, be bound by obedience to present him to the custos who is nearest to the place where they have found him. And the custos shall be strictly bound, by obedience, to guard him strongly day and night as a prisoner so that he cannot be snatched from his hands until he shall personally place him in the hands of his minister. And the minister shall be firmly bound by obedience to send him by such brothers as shall watch him day and night like a prisoner until they shall present him to the Lord of Ostia, who is master protector, and corrector of this brotherhood.[1]

And let not the brothers say : This is another Rule ; for this is a remembrance, a warning, and an exhortation and my Testament which I, little Brother Francis, make for you, my blessed brothers, in order that we may observe in a more Catholic way the Rule which we have promised to the Lord. And let the minister general and all the other ministers and custodes be bound by

[1] Cardinal Ugolino, afterward Gregory IX, was then Bishop of Ostia, and Protector of the Order.

obedience not to add to these words or to take from them. And let them always have this writing with them beside the Rule. And in all the Chapters they hold, when they read the Rule let them read these words also. And I strictly enjoin on all my brothers, clerics and laics, by obedience, not to put glosses on the Rule or on these words saying: Thus they ought to be understood; but as the Lord has given me to speak and to write the Rule and these words simply and purely, so shall you understand them simply and purely[1] and with holy operation observe them until the end.

And whoever shall observe these things[2] may he be filled in heaven with the blessing of the Most High Father and may he be filled on earth with blessing of His Beloved Son together with the Holy Ghost, the Paraclete, and all the Powers of heaven and all the saints. And I, Brother Francis, your little one and servant, in so far as I am able, I confirm to you within and without this most holy blessing.[3]   Amen.[4]

[1] Cod. As. and *Mon.* for "purely" read "without gloss;" *Firm.* and Wadd. add "without gloss."

[2] Cod. An. and O. read "this" for "these things."

[3] Cod. O. adds "to him who caused these words to be written, be all honor, all praise and glory forever and ever."

[4] See 1 Cel. 38, for the blessing given by St. Francis on his deathbed to Elias and the Order.

VII.

Of Living Religiously in a Hermitage.

We learn from St. Bonaventure[1] and the *Fioretti*[2] that as companions began to flock to St. Francis, the man of God hesitated for a while between adopting a life of prayer or of preaching. Although, as we know, he finally decided in favor of the apostolate, yet withal he never altogether separated the contemplative from the active life. A precious witness to this fact is found in the Regulation for the brothers during their sojourn in hermitages with which we are now concerned. To understand the scope of this peculiar piece of legislation, it must be borne in mind that at the beginning of the Franciscan movement the friars had no settled domicile.[3] The wide world was their cloister.[4] Possessing nothing they wandered about like children careless of the day, teaching or preaching, passing the night in hay-lofts or under church

[1] See Bonav. *Leg. Maj.*, XII, 1, where the Saint is represented as discoursing on the relative merits and advantages of the active and contemplative life. Wadding gives this discourse among the Monastic Conferences he attributes to St. Francis. See *Opuscula*, Coll. XIV, p. 318.

[2] See *Floretum S. Francisci*, ed. Sabatier, cap. 16, p. 60. This chapter, which is one of the most interesting from a critical point of view, represents St. Francis as consulting St. Clare and Brother Sylvester on the subject of his doubt.

[3] See First Rule, chap. vii (above, p. 40); also *Speculum Perf.*, ed. Sabatier, pp. 25–26.

[4] As is most poetically described by the author of the *Sacrum Commercium*. Show me your cloister, asks the Lady Poverty of the friars. And they, leading her to the summit of a hill, showed her the wide world, saying: This is our cloister, O Lady Poverty. (See *The Lady Poverty*, by M. Carmichael, p. 128.)

porches, in lazarettos, or deserted huts and grottoes.[1]
The need of having some kind of permanent retreat
where they might retire at times to pray or rest, re-
sulted in the institution of hermitages. These little
solitudes, to which Francis loved to withdraw, may
be found wherever the Saint went. The Celle near
Cortona, the Carceri on Mount Subasio, Greccio in
the valley of Rieti, and the more solitary hermitages,
like Lo Speco, form, as some one has said, a series
of documents, about St. Francis' life, quite as important as the written ones. And not a little of his
spirit still lingers in such of these hermitages as yet
remain. It was for the government of small *loci*[2]
like these that the present special little Rule was
written. Its attribution to St. Francis has not been
questioned. The quaint simplicity of its conception
proclaims its authenticity, and in none of the codices
does it bear the name of any other author than St.
Francis. It may have been written about 1217 ; its
composition certainly belongs to the first decade of
the Order.

In the ancient collections of St. Francis' writings
found in the codices at Florence (Ognissanti), Foligno, Rome (St. Isidore's MS. ½s and the Vatican
MS. 7650), as well as in copies of the compilation
which begins *Fac secundum exemplar*, this Instruction is found at the end of the Admonitions. But in
the greater number of the early codices the Admonitions close as in the present translation, and the

---

[1] See 1 Cel. 1, 17; and *Leg. III Soc.* 55. Such grottoes may
still be seen in St. Francis' country ; they serve as a shelter
for beggars and gypsies.
[2] St. Francis habitually uses the word *locus* or place to
designate the habitations of the friars (see above, Rule II,
chap. vi, p. 68).

opuscule on hermitages is preferably separated from
them, as it is in the Assisian codex and that of St.
Isidore's, Rome (MS. ⅓₃). The text which follows is
based on the Assisi MS., which has been collated
with that of Ognissanti and those at St. Isidore's and
with the version of this Regulation given by Bartholomew of Pisa in his *Conformities*.[1] Here is the text :

OF LIVING RELIGIOUSLY IN A HERMITAGE.

Let those who wish to live religiously in hermitages, be three brothers or four at most. Let
two of them be mothers and have two sons, or
at least one. Let the two former lead the life
of Martha and the other two the life of Mary
Magdalene.[2]

Let those who lead the life of Mary have one
cloister[3] and each his own place, so that they
may not live or sleep together. And let them
always say Compline of the day toward sunset,[4]
and let them be careful to keep silence and to say
their Hours and to rise for Matins, and let them

---

[1] See "Franciscus in admonitionibus suis " (fruct. xii,
P. 11, cap. 30). It was from this text that Wadding took the
Regulation for his edition of the *Opuscula* in which it figures
under the heading *Collationes Monasticae III.*

[2] The figure which presents Mary and Martha as types of
the contemplative and active life was already a familiar one.
See Gregor., *VI Moral.*, c. 37, n. 61 : " Quid per Mariam,
quae verba Domini residens audiebat, nisi contemplativa vita
exprimitur ? Quid per Martham exterioribus obsequiis occu
patam nisi activa vita signatur ? "

[3] Cod. As. after cloister reads : "in which each one shall
have his own cell."

[4] Cod. As. reads : " immediately after sunset."

seek first " the kingdom of God and His justice."[1]
And let them say Prime and Tierce at the proper
time, and, after the hour of Tierce, they may
break silence and may speak and, when it is
pleasing to them, they may go to their mothers
and may ask an alms from them for the love of
the Lord God, like little poor ones.[2]   And after
that, let them say Sext and Nones and Vespers
at the appointed time.

And they must not allow any[3] person to enter
into the cloister where they live, or let them eat
there.   Let those brothers who are mothers
endeavor to keep apart from every person and,
by the obedience of their custos, let them guard
their sons from every person, so that no one may
speak with them.   And let these sons not speak
with any person except with their mothers and
with their custos, when it shall please him to
visit them with the blessing of God.[4]   But the
sons must sometimes in turn assume the office
of mothers, for a time, according as it may seem
to them to dispose.   Let them strive to observe
all the above diligently and earnestly.[5]

[1] Luke 12 : 31.
[2] This is the reading of the Cod. As. and Is.; other texts
read the " poorest beggars."
[3] Cod. O. adds : " any woman or person whatsoever."
[4] The text in Cod. As. ends here.
[5] See 2 Cel. 3, 113.

PART II.

SIX LETTERS OF ST. FRANCIS

THE LETTERS OF ST. FRANCIS.

O F the seventeen letters attributed to St. Francis in Wadding's edition of the *Opuscula*, five cannot be admitted as genuine, at least in the form given in that work, and the rest need, with two exceptions, to be reclassified.

In the first category, we must place the familiar letter in which St. Francis gives St. Antony permission to teach theology (Epistle III, in Wadding's edition), and which has been excluded by the Quaracchi editors as doubtful on the ground that it exists in too many different forms.[1] The letters to Brother Elias, to the Provincial Ministers, and to the Custodes (Epistles VII, IX, and XIV, in Wadding's edition), were translated by Wadding into Latin from a Spanish text,[2] and have not come down to us in their original form. Hence they do not figure in the Quaracchi edition. Neither does the letter (Epis. XVII, in Wadding's edition) to "Brother" Giacoma dei Settisoli, which is clearly an extract from Chapter XVIII of the *Actus B. Francisci et Sociorum ejus*.[3] Following the

[1] On this letter see Appendix.
[2] Wadding drew on the Spanish text of Rebolledo (*Chron*, P. I, l. II, c. xxvii) and himself appears to have had misgivings, at least as regards the authenticity of Epistle VII.
[3] See *Actus B. Francisci*, etc., ed. Sabatier, p. 63. M. Sabatier attributes the authorship of this compilation (which contains, as is now known, among other matters, the original Latin text of the traditional *Fioretti*) to Fra Ugolino di Monte Giorgio, and believes its date to be between 1280 and 1320. It is, however, from Thomas of Celano that we know St.

Quaracchi editors, I have excluded these five letters from the present work.

As regards the reclassification of the other letters attributed to St. Francis by Wadding, Epistles IV, V, and XIII in his edition are without doubt genuine writings of St. Francis, but they are not letters ; at least, the oldest MSS. do not give them in epistolary form. The two former are fragments of a "rule of life" and a "last wish," written by St. Francis for St. Clare ; No. XIII is an Instruction on the Blessed Sacrament. All three are given elsewhere in the present volume in their proper form.[1] For the rest, the Epistles numbered I and II by Wadding form the text of one and the same letter " To all the Faithful;" those numbered VI and VIII seem to be a summary of the genuine letter "To a Minister," and No. X is part of the letter " To the General Chapter" also given below, while Epistles XI and XII form but one letter in the oldest codices and belong to this same letter to the General Chapter. The only two letters, then, of St. Francis which, both as regards matter and form, may be accepted as Wadding gives them, are numbers VIII and XV, addressed to the

Francis to have written a letter to the Lady Giacoma (See *Tr. de Miraculis* in *Anal. Bolland.*, t. xviii). See also *Spec. Perf.* (ed. Sabatier), c. XII, for reference to this letter. The narrative of Celano renders the text of the letter given in the *Actus* very doubtful. The fact that the expression " St. Mary of the Angels " is used in it to designate the Portiuncula is in itself sufficient to militate against its authenticity. Neither St. Francis nor his companions ever employed this term ; they invariably said "St. Mary of the Portiuncula." Any document, therefore, containing the former expression bespeaks a fourteenth century origin at earliest. See *Frère Jacqueline: Recherches Historiques*, by Fr. Edouard d'Alençon, Paris, 1899.

[1] See above, pp. 23, 77, 78.

Rulers and to Brother Leo respectively. In a word, as a result of this process of elimination and reclassification, only five of the seventeen letters ascribed to St. Francis by Wadding remain to us, namely :—

1. *Letter to all the Faithful* (Ep. I and II of Wadding).

2. *Letter to the General Chapter* (Ep. X, XI, and XII of Wadding).

3. *Letter to a Minister* (Ep. VI and VIII of Wadding).

4. *Letter to the Rulers* (Ep. XV of Wadding).

5. *Letter to Brother Leo* (Ep. XVI of Wadding).

To these five letters, the Quaracchi editors have added the undoubtedly authentic letter of St. Francis to the Custodes,[1] making six in all. Such are the six letters which I have here rendered into English. Let us now consider each of them in order.

---

[1] The letter which Wadding translated from the Spanish, under this title and numbered XIV, appears to have been an incomplete version of the letter here given in full.

I.

LETTER TO ALL THE FAITHFUL.

The authenticity of this letter has never been called into question. The text itself and the consensus of codices alike bespeak its genuineness. Its inspiration is, as the Quaracchi editors have pointed out, kindred to that of St. Francis' other writings. Moreover, many of the sentiments contained in this letter, written in great part in the words of the Gospel, are expressed by the Saint in almost the self-same language in the Rules and elsewhere.[1]

In the spring of 1215, St. Francis suffered again from an attack of fever similar to that which had prostrated him in Spain. It was then, his biographers tell us,[2] that the Saint, unable as he was to preach, was moved by the zeal that devoured him, to put his message into writing. As a result we have this the first and longest of his letters, addressed to all the Faithful,—a precious example of his far-reaching solicitude and all embracing sympathy. There is a simplicity in the superscription and opening words of this letter characteristic of the Middle Ages. Then was the time when men believed that if they had a good idea or a deep feeling on any subject, the world at large had but to learn of this idea or feeling and it would immediately adopt it. It was thus that some bishops of the south of France, having established

[1] Compare for example the passage on p. 101, beginning "Let us therefore love God," etc., with Chapter XXII of the First Rule (p. 58); and the prayer of Christ given on p. 105, with the conclusion of the same chapter (p. 59).

[2] See Le Monnier, *l. c.*, p. 202, and Knox Little, *l. c.*, p. 164. Wadding, *Annales*, ad. an. 1213, places the writing of this letter two or three years earlier, which seems less probable.

the Truce of God, wrote "to all the archbishops, bishops, priests and clerics inhabiting all Italy" to recommend to them "this new method come from heaven" of reëstablishing and fixing peace among men. Even so Dante, in the excess of his grief, wrote "to all the princes of the earth" to make known to them that, in losing Beatrice, "the earth had lost its spring and the future of the world was threatened."[1] Thus too St. Francis undertook in the present letter to recall "to all the Christians who are in the whole world," those eternal truths which are ever old and ever new, convinced as he was that the world must needs walk in their light if it only realized them more. For the rest, as has been remarked, the description it contains of the death of a rich man is, from a literary point of view, rightly considered the most carefully composed bit of St. Francis' writing that has come down to us.

A fragment containing this realistic picture was published in 1900 by M. Sabatier,[2] who believed it to be a new and complete opuscule of St. Francis. But the very *Incipit* of the piece, "The body grows feeble, death approaches . . ." and the *Explicit*, "dies a bitter death," clearly show that, with the exception of a few words at the opening, this "nouveau opuscule" is nothing more or less than an extract from St. Francis' letter to all the Faithful.

Wadding, as I have already noted, following the lead of Rodolfo di Tossignano,[3] unskilfully divided this letter into two distinct epistles (I and II in his

---

[1] See Le Monnier, *l. c.*, p. 203. To him I am indebted for these quotations.

[2] See his edition of Bartholi, *Tractatus*, Appendix, p. 132 seq.

[3] See *Historiarum Seraphicae Religionis libri tres* (Venice, 1586), fol. 174 r, for that part of the letter which Wadding gives as *Epistola I.*

edition). He has also distributed the letter into twelve chapters with separate titles. No doubt he was justified in doing so by the example of some codices, but the Quaracchi editors, following the best MSS., have omitted this division and it will not be found in the present translation.[1]

The letter to all the Faithful may be found entire in seventeen of the codices mentioned above, to wit, those at *Assisi* (fol. 23); *Berlin* (fol. 105); *Florence* (Ognissanti MS., fol. 7); *St. Floriano* (fol. 36); *Foligno* (fol. 25); *Lemberg* (fol. 341); *Liegnitz* (fol. 136); *Munich* (fol. 31); *Oxford* (fol. 98); *Paris* (Maz. MS. 1743, fol. 137; Maz. MS. 989, fol. 193; Prot. theol. fac. MS., fol. 88); *Rome* (St. Isidore's MSS. ½₅, fol. 18 and ¼ , fol. 15; Vatican MSS. 4354, fol. 43, and 7650, fol. 16), and at *Düsseldorf* (cod. B 132, fol. not numbered).

Fragments of the letter may also be found in the codices at *Luttich* (fol. 158); *Naples* (F. 24, fol. 107), and *Volterra* (fol. 148).[2] For the text contained in the Quaracchi edition, the editors took as a basis the MSS. of Assisi and Ognissanti, collating these with the codices at St. Isidore's and with the versions of the letter given in the *Monumenta* (tract II, fol. 278 r) and the *Conformities* (fruct. XII, P. 11).[3] It is the Quaracchi text that I have here translated as follows:

I.—LETTER TO ALL THE FAITHFUL.

To all Christians, religious, clerics, and laics, men and women, to all who dwell in the whole

---

[1] It has been adopted in the new French edition of St. Francis' works. See *Opuscules*, pp. 122–135.

[2] It was from this fourteenth century MS. that M. Sabatier edited as a new opuscule the fragment above mentioned.

[3] Bartholomew of Pisa here inserts the greater part of the letter *passim*.

world, Brother Francis, their servant and subject, presents reverent homage, wishing true peace from heaven and sincere charity in the Lord.

Being the servant of all, I am bound to serve all and to administer the balm-bearing words of my Lord.[1] Wherefore, considering in my mind that, because of the infirmity and weakness of my body, I cannot visit each one personally, I propose by this present letter and message[2] to offer you the words of our Lord Jesus Christ who is the Word of the Father and the words of the Holy Ghost which are "spirit and life."[3]

This Word of the Father, so worthy, so holy and glorious, whose coming the most High Father announced from heaven by His holy archangel Gabriel to the holy and glorious Virgin Mary[4] in whose womb He received the true flesh of our humanity and frailty, He, being rich[5] above all, willed, nevertheless, with His most Blessed Mother, to choose poverty.

And when His Passion was nigh, He celebrated the Pasch with His disciples and, taking bread, He gave thanks and blessed and broke saying: Take ye and eat: this is My Body. And, taking the chalice, He said: This is My Blood of the New Testament, which shall be shed for you and for many unto remission of

---

[1] Cod. O. reads: "all the words of the Lord."
[2] Cod. O. reads: "by this present letter and now."
[3] John 6: 64.
[4] See Luke 1: 31.
[5] See II Cor. 8: 9.

sins.[1] After that He prayed to the Father, saying : " Father, if it be possible, let this chalice pass from Me." [2] " And His sweat became as drops of blood, trickling down upon the ground." [3] But withal, He gave up His will to the will of the Father, saying : Father, Thy will be done : not as I will, but as Thou wilt.[4] Such was the will of the Father that His Son, Blessed and Glorious, whom He gave to us, and who was born for us,[5] should by His own Blood, sacrifice, and oblation, offer Himself on the altar of the Cross, not for Himself, by whom " all things were made," [6] but for our sins, leaving us an example that we should follow His steps.[7] And He wishes that we should all be saved by Him [8] and that we should receive Him with a pure heart and a chaste body. But there are few who wish to receive Him and to be saved by Him, although His yoke is sweet and His burden light.[9]

Those who will not taste how sweet the Lord is [10] and who love darkness rather than the light,[11] not wishing to fulfil the commandments of God are cursed : of them it is said by the prophet : " They are cursed who decline from Thy commandments." [12] But, O how happy and blessed

---

[1] See Matt. 26 : 26-28; Luke 22 : 19-20; I Cor. 11 : 24-25.

[2] Matt. 26 : 39.   [3] Luke 22 : 44.

[4] See Matt. 26: 42 and 39.

[5] Cod. O. omits : "and was born for us."

[6] John 1 : 3.   [7] See I Peter 2 : 21.

[8] Cod. O. omits : "And He wishes that we should all be saved by Him."

[9] See Matt. 11 : 30.   [10] See Ps. 33 : 9.

[11] See John 3 : 19.   [12] Ps. 118 : 21.

are those who love the Lord, who do as the Lord Himself says in the Gospel : "Thou shalt love the Lord thy God with thy whole heart and with thy whole soul and . . . thy neighbor as thyself."[1] Let us therefore love God and adore Him with a pure heart and a pure mind because He Himself, seeking that above all, says : "The true adorers shall adore the Father in spirit and in truth."[2] For all who "adore Him must adore Him in spirit and in truth."[3] And let us offer Him praises and prayers day and night, saying : "Our Father who art in heaven," for "we ought always to pray, and not to faint."[4]

We ought indeed to confess all our sins to a priest and receive from him the Body and Blood of our Lord Jesus Christ.[5] He who does not eat His Flesh and does not drink His Blood cannot enter into the Kingdom of God.[6] Let him, however, eat and drink worthily, because he who receives unworthily "eateth and drinketh judgment to himself, not discerning the Body of the Lord,"[7]—that is, not discerning it from other foods.

Let us, moreover, "bring forth fruits worthy of penance."[8] And let us love our neighbors as ourselves, and, if any one does not wish to

---

[1] Matt. 22 : 37-39.   [2] John 4 : 23.
[3] John 4 : 24.   [4] Luke 18 : 1.
[5] Cod. O. adds : "For the Lord says, who does not eat," etc.
[6] See John 6 : 54.   [7] I Cor. 11 : 29.
[8] Luke 3 : 8.

love them as himself or cannot,[1] let him at least do them not harm, but let him do good to them.

Let those who have received the power of judging others, exercise judgment with mercy,[2] as they hope to obtain mercy from the Lord. For let judgment without mercy be shown to him that doth not mercy.[3] Let us then have charity and humility and let us give alms because they wash souls from the foulness of sins.[4] For men lose all which they leave in this world ; they carry with them, however, the reward of charity and alms which they have given, for which they shall receive a recompense and worthy remuneration from the Lord.

We ought also to fast and to abstain from vices and sins[5] and from superfluity of food and drink, and to be Catholics. We ought also to visit Churches frequently and to reverence clerics not only for themselves, if they are sinners, but on account of their office and administration of the most holy Body and Blood of our Lord Jesus Christ, which they sacrifice on the altar and receive and administer to others. And let us all know for certain that no one can be saved except by the Blood of our Lord Jesus Christ and by the holy words of the Lord which clerics say and announce and distribute and they alone administer and not others. But religious

---

[1] Cod. As. and editions omit " or cannot."
[2] Cod. O. reads : " judgment and mercy."
[3] See Jas. 2 : 13. [4] See Tob. 4 : 11.
[5] See Eccli. 3 : 32.

especially, who have renounced the world, are bound to do more and greater things, but "not to leave the other undone."[1]

We ought to hate our bodies with [their] vices and sins, because the Lord says in the Gospel that all vices and sins come forth from the heart.[2] We ought to love our enemies and do good to them that hate us.[3] We ought to observe the precepts and counsels of our Lord Jesus Christ. We ought also to deny ourselves and to put our bodies beneath the yoke of servitude and holy obedience as each one has promised to the Lord. And let no man be bound by obedience to obey any one in that where sin or offence is committed.

But let him to whom obedience has been entrusted and who is considered greater become as the lesser[4] and the servant of the other brothers, and let him show and have the mercy toward each of his brothers that he would wish to be shown to himself if he were in the like situation. And let him not be angry with a brother on account of his offence, but let him advise him kindly and encourage him with all patience and humility.

We ought not to be "wise according to the flesh"[5] and prudent, but we ought rather to be simple, humble, and pure. And let us hold our bodies in dishonor and contempt because through our fault we are all wretched and cor-

---

[1] Luke 11: 42.
[2] See Matt. 15: 18–19.
[3] See Luke 6: 27.
[4] See Luke 22: 26.
[5] I Cor. 1: 26.

rupt, foul and worms, as the Lord says by the prophet: "I am a worm and no man, the reproach of men and the outcast of the people."[1] We should never desire to be above others, but ought rather to be servants and subject "to every human creature for God's sake."[2]   And the spirit of the Lord[3] shall rest upon all those who do these things and who shall persevere to the end, and He shall make His abode and dwelling in them,[4] and they shall be children of the heavenly Father[5] whose works they do, and they are the spouses, brothers and mothers of our Lord Jesus Christ. We are spouses when by the Holy Ghost the faithful soul is united to Jesus Christ. We are His brothers when we do the will of His Father who is in heaven.[6] We are His mothers when we bear Him in our heart and in our body through pure love and a clean conscience and we bring Him forth by holy work which ought to shine as an example to others.

O how glorious and holy and great to have a Father in heaven ! O how holy, fair, and lovable to have a spouse in heaven ![7]   O how holy and how beloved, well pleasing and humble, peaceful and sweet and desirable above all to have such a brother who has laid down His life for His sheep,[8] and who has prayed for us to the Father,

[1] Ps. 21 : 7.
[2] I Peter 2 : 13.
[3] See Is. 11 : 2.
[4] See John 14 : 23.
[5] See Matt. 5 : 45.
[6] See Matt. 12 : 50.
[7] Cod. As. and that of Volterra with the *Mon.* add : "the Paraclete."
[8] See John 10 : 15.

saying : Father, keep them in Thy Name whom
Thou hast given Me. Father, all those whom
Thou hast given Me in the world were Thine,
and Thou hast given them to Me. And the
words which Thou gavest Me I have given to
them ; and they have received them, and have
known in very deed that I came forth from Thee,
and they have believed that Thou didst send Me.
I pray for them: not for the world : bless and
sanctify them. And for them I sanctify Myself
that they may be sanctified in one as We also
are. And I will, Father, that where I am, they
also may be with Me, that they may see My
glory in My kingdom.[1]

And since He has suffered so many things for
us and has done and will do so much good to us,
let every creature which is in heaven and on
earth and in the sea and in the abysses render
praise to God and glory and honor and benediction ;[2] for He is our strength and power who
alone is good,[3] alone most high, alone almighty
and admirable, glorious and alone holy, praiseworthy and blessed without end forever and
ever. Amen.

But all those who do not do penance and who
do not receive the Body and Blood of our Lord
Jesus Christ, but who give themselves to vices
and sins and walk after evil concupiscence and
bad desires and who do not observe what they
have promised, corporally they serve the world

[1] See John 17 : 6–24.   [2] See Apoc. 5 : 13.
[3] See Luke 18 : 19.

and its fleshly desires and cares and solicitudes
for this life, but mentally they serve the devil,
deceived by him whose sons they are and whose
works they do; blind they are because they see
not the true light,—our Lord Jesus Christ. They
have no spiritual wisdom, for they have not in
them the Son of God who is the true wisdom of
the Father: of these it is said: "their wisdom
was swallowed up."[1] They know, understand, and
do evil and wittingly lose their souls. Beware,
ye blind, deceived by your enemies—to wit, by the
world, the flesh and by the devil—for it is sweet
to the body to commit sin and bitter to serve
God because all vices and sins come forth and
proceed from the heart of man, as it is said in
the Gospel.[2]

And you have nothing of good in this world
or in the future. You think to possess for long
the vanities of this world, but you are deceived;
for a day and an hour will come of which you
think not and do not know and are ignorant of.
The body grows feeble, death approaches, neighbors and friends come saying: "Put your affairs
in order." And his wife and his children, neighbors and friends, make believe to weep. And
looking, he sees them weeping and is moved by
a bad emotion, and thinking within himself he
says: "Behold, I place my soul and body and my
all in your hands." Verily, that man is cursed
who confides and exposes his soul and body and
his all in such hands. Wherefore, the Lord

[1] Ps. 106: 27.   [2] See Matt. 15: 19.

says by the prophet : " Cursed be the man that trusteth in man." [1] And at once they cause a priest to come and the priest says to him : " Wilt thou do penance for all thy sins ? " He answers : " I will." " Wilt thou from thy sub-stance, as far as thou canst, satisfy for what thou hast done and for the things in which thou hast defrauded and deceived men." [2] He answers : " No."—And the priest says : " Why not ? "— " Because I have put everything into the hands of my relatives and friends." And he begins to lose the power of speech and thus this miserable man dies a bitter death.[3]

But let all know that wheresoever or howso-ever a man may die in criminal sin, without satisfaction—when he could satisfy and did not satisfy—the devil snatches his soul from his body with such violence and anguish as no one can know except him who suffers it. And all talent and power, learning and wisdom [4] that he thought to possess are taken from him.[5] And his relatives and friends take to themselves his substance and divide it and say afterwards : " Cursed be his soul because he could have ac-quired and given us more than he did, and did

---

[1] Jer. 17 : 5.

[2] Cod. O. and Pis. read : " Wilt thou satisfy for the things taken unjustly,—that is, those things by which thou hast cheated thy neighbor."

[3] Cod. As. and *Mon.* omit : " a bitter death." Cod. Pis. and Volterra omit " miserable man."

[4] Cod. As. and *Mon.* omit " wisdom."

[5] See Luke 8 : 18.

not acquire it." But the worms eat his body. And thus he loses soul and body in this short life and goes into hell, where he shall be tormented without end.

In the Name of the Father and of the Son and of the Holy Ghost. Amen.[1] All to whom this letter may come, I, Brother Francis, your little servant, pray and conjure you by the charity which God is,[2] and with the will to kiss your feet, to receive these balm-bearing words[3] of our Lord Jesus Christ with humility and charity and to put them in practice kindly and to observe them perfectly.[4] And let those who do not know how to read have them read often and let them keep them by them with holy operation unto the end, for they are spirit and life.[5] And those who do not do this shall render an account on the day of Judgment before the tribunal of Christ. And all those who shall receive them kindly and understand them and send them to others as example, if they persevere in them unto the end,[6] may the Father and the Son and the Holy Ghost bless them. Amen.

[1] These words are not found except in Cod. As., which omits the following sentence : "All to whom this letter may come."

[2] See I John 4: 16.

[3] Cod. As. and *Mon.* read : "that these words and others."

[4] Cod. As. and *Mon.* omit what follows up to "And all those."

[5] See John 6: 64.

[6] See Matt. 10: 22.

II.

LETTER TO ALL THE FRIARS.

It was at the end of his days[1] when he was ill,[2] that St. Francis wrote this letter to the Minister General and to all the Friars. In it he confesses all his sins to God, to the Saints and to the Friars, and in weighty words urges once again what was ever uppermost in his mind and heart : reverence toward the Blessed Sacrament, observance of the Rule and the Divine Office. The same desires and counsels contained in this letter may also be found in the Testament, and there is little doubt that both works were composed about the same time.

This letter, like the preceding one, was wrongly divided by Rodolfo di Tossignano.[3] Wadding following suit, made three separate epistles out of it,[4] an error all the more remarkable since Bartholomew of Pisa in his *Conformities* (fruct. xii, P. 11, n. 47) and before him Ubertino da Casale in the *Arbor Vitae* (l. v, c. vii, fol. 224) had edited the text correctly. Moreover, this useless division, which is not called for by the context of the letter but is rather in conflict with it, is not found in any of the early MS. collections containing St. Francis' writings.

The letter to all the Friars may be found in fourteen of the MSS. mentioned above as containing the letter to all the Faithful, to wit, those of Assisi, Düs-

[1] So Ubertino da Casale tells us in his *Arbor Vitae*, finished on Mount La Verna, September 28, 1305 (l. v, cap. vii).

[2] As we learn from the rubric in the Assisi MS. 338 : " De lictera et ammonitione beatissimi patris nostri Francisci quam misit fratribus ad capitulum quando erat infirmus."

[3] *Hist. Seraph.*, fol. 173 v.

[4] Epistles X, XI, and XII in his edition.

seldorf, Florence (Ognissanti), St. Floriano, Foligno,
Liegnitz, Munich, Oxford, Paris (all three MSS.), and
Rome (both MSS. at St. Isidore's and cod. 4354 of
the Vatican library). It is also contained in eight
other codices : (1) *Capistran* (munic. lib. cod. xxii,
fol. 85 r); (2) *Freiburg* in Switzerland (lib. ad Conventual Conv., cod. 23, l. 60); (3) *Paris* (nat. lib. cod.
18327, fol. 159 v); (4–5) *Subiaco* (monast. lib. cod.
120, fol. 325 and 212, fol. 184); (6–7) *Rome* (St. Antony's cod., fol. 61 r and 80 r, and Vatic. lib., cod. B.
82, fol. 147 v); (8) *Volterra* (Guarnacci lib., cod. 225,
fol. 151 r). Of these last named codices, the two
Roman MSS. and that of Volterra date from the fourteenth century; the other five from the fifteenth.

For the Quaracchi text of the letter, which is here
translated, the MSS. of Assisi,[1] St. Antony's, Ognissanti, and St. Isidore's, were collated with the versions of it given in the *Arbor Vitae* (l. v, cap. vii,
fol. 224 v), *Monumenta* (fol. 281 v) and *Firmamenta*
(fol. 21 r).[2] It may be noted that in placing the prayer,
"Almighty, Eternal God," etc., at the end of the
letter, the Quaracchi editors have followed the order
of the Assisian, Antonian, Liegnitz, and both Mazarin
MSS.[3] But enough by the way of introduction to
Letter II, which St. Francis addressed :—

---

[1] Following this MS., Mgr. Faloci edited the first part of the
letter (to "world without end. Amen,"—see page 116) in his
Miss. Frances, t. VI, p. 94.

[2] The *Mon.* and *Firm.*, like Rodolfo (fol. 173 v), give
only the first part of the letter, which Wadding makes Epis.
XII.

[3] It is placed immediately before the letter in the other family
of MSS. mentioned in the Introduction, to which the Ognissanti
MS. belongs.

TO ALL THE FRIARS.

In the name of the Highest Trinity and Holy Unity of the Father and of the Son and of the Holy Ghost. Amen.[1]

To all the reverend and much beloved brothers, to[2] the minister general of the Order of Minors, its lord, and to the other ministers general who shall come after him, and to all the ministers and custodes and priests of the same brotherhood, humble in Christ, and to all the simple and obedient brothers, the first and the last, Brother Francis, a mean and fallen man, your little servant, gives greeting in Him who has redeemed and washed us in His Precious Blood,[3] and whom when you hear His Name adore ye with fear and reverence, prostrate on the ground;[4] the Lord Jesus Christ, such is the Name[5] of the most High Son, blessed forever.   Amen.

---

[1] Cod. As. omits this invocation.

[2] Cod. As. adds " to Brother *A*, minister general." It has been surmised that St. Francis wished this letter to be read at the opening of all subsequent chapters, with a view to perpetuating his spiritual presence among the brothers.   In this hypothesis, the copyist was supposed to fill in here the initial of the minister general governing the order at the time he wrote.   The fact that *A* is the initial given at the head of the Assisian MS. may afford a clue to the date of its composition (Albert of Pisa governed the order 1239-40, and *A*ymon of Faversham, 1240-44), but in the body of the letter (see below, p. 117) the minister general is referred to as Brother *H* [*H*elias (?) 1232-39].   Cod. An. at the head of the letter reads Brother *T* [*T*homas of Farignano (?), 1367-73].

[3] See Apoc. 1 : 5.   [4] See Gen. 19: 1 and elsewhere.

[5] See Luke 1: 32.

Hear, my lords, my sons and my brothers, and with your ears receive my words.[1] Incline the ear[2] of your heart and obey the voice of the Son of God. Keep His commandments with all your heart and fulfil His counsels with a perfect mind. Praise Him for He is good[3] and extol Him in your works,[4] for therefore He has sent you through all the world that by word and deed you may bear witness to His voice,[5] and you may make known to all that there is no other Almighty besides Him.[6] Persevere under discipline[7] and obedience and with a good and firm purpose fulfil what you have promised Him. The Lord God offers Himself to you as to His sons.[8]

Wherefore, brothers, kissing your feet and with the charity of which I am capable, I conjure you all to show all reverence and all honor possible to the most holy Body and Blood of our Lord Jesus Christ, in whom the things that are in heaven and the things that are on earth are pacified and reconciled to Almighty God.[9] I also beseech in the Lord all my brothers who are and shall be and desire to be priests[10] of the Most High that, when they wish to celebrate Mass, being pure, they offer the true Sacrifice

---

[1] See Acts 2 : 14.   [2] See Isa. 55 : 3.
[3] See Ps. 135 : 1.   [4] See Tob. 13 : 6.
[5] Cod. An. reads: "you may make all stand dumbfounded who oppose Him in word or deed."
[6] See Tob. 13 : 4.   [7] See Heb. 12 : 7.
[8] See Heb. 12 : 7.   [9] See Col. 1 : 20.
[10] The word priests is added in Cod. As., and by Ubertino.

of the Body and Blood of our Lord Jesus Christ
purely, with reverence, with a holy and clean
intention, not for any earthly thing or fear or
for the love of any man, as it were pleasing
men.[1] But let every will, in so far as the grace
of the Almighty helps, be directed to Him,[2]
desiring thence to please the High Lord Himself alone because He alone works there [in the
Holy Sacrifice] as it may please Him, for He
Himself says: " Do this for a commemoration of
Me ;"[3] if any one doth otherwise he becomes
the traitor Judas[4] and is made guilty of the
Body and Blood of the Lord.[5]

Call to mind, priests, my brothers, what is
written in the law of Moses: how those trans-
gressing even materially died by the decree of
the Lord without any mercy.[6] How much more
and worse punishments he deserves to suffer
"who hath trodden under foot the Son of God
and hath esteemed the Blood of the testament
unclean by which he was sanctified and hath
offered an affront to the spirit of grace."[7] For
man despises, soils, and treads under foot the
Lamb of God when, as the Apostle says,[8] not
discerning and distinguishing the holy bread of
Christ from other nourishments or works, he

---

[1] See Eph. 6: 6, and Col. 3: 22.

[2] Cod. As. reads: "to the Lord."

[3] Luke 22: 19.

[4] Cod. O., *Mon.*, and *Firm.*, with Ubertino, omit the rest of
this sentence.

[5] See I Cor. 11: 27.   [6] See Heb. 10: 28.

[7] Heb. 10: 29.   [8] See I Cor. 11: 29.

either eats unworthily or, if he be worthy, he
eats in vain and unbecomingly since the Lord
has said by the prophet : Cursed be the man that
doth the work of the Lord deceitfully.[1] And
He condemns the priests who will not take this
to heart saying : " I will curse your blessings." [2]

Hear ye, my brothers : If the Blessed Virgin
Mary is so honored, as is meet, because she bore
Him in [her] most holy womb ; if the blessed
Baptist trembled and did not dare to touch the
holy forehead of God ; if the sepulchre in which
He lay for some time, is venerated, how holy,
just, and worthy ought he to be who touches
with his hands, who receives with his heart and
his mouth, and proffers to be received by others
Him who is now no more to die but to triumph
in a glorified eternity : on whom the angels desire to look.[3]

Consider your dignity, brothers, priests, and
be holy because He Himself is holy.[4] And as
the Lord God has honored you above all through
this mystery, even so do you also love and reverence and honor Him above all. It is a great
misery and a deplorable weakness when you
have Him thus present to care for anything else
in the whole world. Let the entire man be
seized with fear ; let the whole world tremble ;
let heaven exult when Christ, the Son of the
Living God, is on the altar in the hands of the
priest. O admirable height and stupendous con-

---

[1] See Jerem. 48 : 10.   [2] Mal. 2 : 2.
[3] See I Pet. 1 : 12.   [4] See Levit. 11 : 44.

descension! O humble sublimity! O sublime humility! that the Lord of the universe, God and the Son of God, so humbles Himself that for our salvation He hides Himself under a morsel of bread. Consider, brothers, the humility of God and "pour out your hearts before Him,"[1] and be ye humbled that ye may be exalted by Him.[2] Do not therefore keep back anything for yourselves that He may receive you entirely who gives Himself up entirely to you.

Wherefore I admonish and exhort in the Lord, that, in the places in which the brothers live, only one Mass be celebrated in the day, according to the form of holy Church.[3] If, however, there be many priests in the place, let one be contented, through love of charity, by hearing the celebration of another priest, for the Lord Jesus Christ replenishes those who are worthy of it, present and absent. He, although He may seem to be present in many places, nevertheless remains undivided and suffers no change ; but One everywhere He works as it may please Him with the Lord God the Father, and the

[1] See Ps. 61 : 9.   [2] See 1 Pet. 5 : 6.

[3] Philip Melanchthon in his Apology (*Augsburg Confession*, art. on the Mass) usurped these words of St. Francis to defend his erroneous teaching against private Masses. But there is nothing in this letter or elsewhere to show that St. Francis reprehended such Masses in any way. On the contrary, as the Bollandists point out, the words "according to the form of holy Church" refer to the rite of the Roman Church to be followed in the celebration of Mass and not to the one Mass to be celebrated daily. (See *Acta S.S.*, t. II, Oct., pp. 998–999).

Holy Ghost the Paraclete, world without end. Amen.

And since " he that is of God heareth the words of God,"[1] we who have been more specially destined for the divine offices, ought, in consequence, not only to hear and do what God says, but also—in order to impress upon ourselves the greatness of our Creator and our subjection to Him—to watch the vessels and other objects which contain His holy words. On that account I warn all my brothers and I strengthen them in Christ, wheresoever they may find the divine written words to venerate them so far as they are able, and if they are not well preserved or if they lie scattered disgracefully in any place, let them, in so far as it concerns them, collect and preserve them, honoring in the words the Lord who has spoken. For many things are sanctified by the word of God,[2] and by the power of the words of Christ the Sacrament of the Altar is effected.

Moreover I confess all my sins to God the Father and to the Son and to the Holy Ghost and to the Blessed Mary ever Virgin and to all the Saints in heaven and on earth and to the minister general of this our religion as to my venerable Lord, and to all the priests of our order and to all my other blessed brothers. I have offended in many ways through my grievous fault, especially because I have not observed the Rule which I have promised to the Lord and

[1] John 8 : 47.   [2] See 1 Tim. 4 : 5.

I have not said the office as prescribed by the Rule either by reason of my negligence or weakness or because I am ignorant and simple. Wherefore, by all means as far as I am able, I beseech my lord, the general minister, to cause the Rule to be inviolably observed by all, and let the clerics say the office with devotion before God, not attending to melody of voice but to harmony of mind, so that the voice may be in accord with the mind and the mind in accord with God, so that they may please God by purity of mind and not coax the ears of the people by voluptuousness of voice. As for myself I promise to keep these things strictly, as the Lord may give me grace, and I leave them to the brothers who are with me to be observed in the office and in the other appointed regulations. But whosoever of the brothers will not observe them, I do not hold them as Catholics or as my brothers and I do not wish either to see them or speak [with them], until they have done penance. I say this also of all others who setting aside the discipline of the Rule, go wandering about; for our Lord Jesus Christ gave His life lest He might lose the obedience of the most Holy Father.[1]

I, Brother Francis, a useless man and unworthy creature of the Lord God, say to Brother Elias, the minister of our whole religion, by our Lord Jesus Christ, and to all the ministers general who shall be after him and to the other custodes

[1] See Philip. 2 : 8.

and guardians of the brothers, who are and shall be, that they have this writing with them, put it in practice and seduously preserve it. And I entreat them to guard jealously those things which are written in it and to cause them to be carefully observed according to the good pleasure of the Almighty God now and ever as long as this world may last.

Blessed be you by the Lord who shall have done these things and may the Lord be with you forever. Amen.

Almighty, eternal, just, and merciful God, give to us wretches to do for Thee what we know Thee to will and to will always that which is pleasing to Thee; so that inwardly purified, inwardly illumined and kindled by the flame of the Holy Ghost, we may be able to follow in the footsteps of Thy Son, our Lord Jesus Christ, and by Thy grace alone come to Thee the Most High, who in perfect Trinity and simple Unity livest and reignest and gloriest God Almighty forever and ever. Amen.[1]

[1] This prayer, which, as I have said, is found in some MSS. at the head and in others at the foot of the present letter, is separated from it altogether by Wadding, who (p. 101) places it immediately after the sheet given by St. Francis to Brother Leo. There it is also found in the new French edition of the *Opuscula* (p. 25).

III.

To a Certain Minister.

The tenor of this letter seems to indicate that it was written before the confirmation of the Second Rule by Pope Honorius;[1] and very likely in the early part of 1223. All the early MSS. attribute it to St. Francis and, as regards both matter and form, it closely resembles the Saint's other writings. There is, however, no small diversity of opinion as to whom it was addressed. But from the wording of the last paragraph of the letter, referring to the chapter: "thou wilt be there with thy brothers," it would appear to have been sent to some provincial minister rather than to the minister general. Moreover, as Professor Goetz rightly remarks,[2] the beginning of the letter implies that this minister had proposed some doubts or difficulties as to the manner of dealing with brothers who had fallen into sin. Hence the abrupt opening of the letter, "I speak to thee on the subject of thy soul," etc., refers to some question which the letter is intended to answer, and from the fact that patience is commended "more than a hermitage," the Quaracchi editors think we might infer that the minister in question was desirous of embracing a solitary life. Be this as it may, I am unable to

[1] It refers to "the chapters which speak of mortal sin" which are only found in the First Rule (see pp. 37, 47, 53), and speaks of proposed changes in the Rule which could not, as is clear, have been made after November, 1223. In particular the subject of the tenth chapter of the new Rule discussed in the Chapter held at Portiuncula, June 11th of that year (see *Spec. Perf.*, ed. Sabatier, c. 1), is mentioned as not yet definitely settled.

[2] See *Quellen*, etc., t.. XXII, p. 547.

agree with M. Sabatier in so far as he finds in this letter "more objurgations and reproaches than counsels."[1]

The letter exists in the Vatican MS. 7650, St. Isidore's MS. 1/25 and the Ognissanti and St. Floriano codices above described. The first part of it may also be found in the National Library at Naples (Cod. XII, F. 32). An abridgment of the Letter is given by Rodolfo ;[2] a different abstract is found in the *Conformities*.[3] In the more complete summary furnished by Wadding,[4] it might be possible with M. Sabatier, and Dr. Lempp,[5] owing to the omission of a large piece of the letter, to read into St. Francis' words the precept that a brother guilty of mortal sin should be absolved without any penance. But with the full text of the letter before us, any such attempt is, needless to say, impossible, as Mr. Carmichael has clearly shown.[6]

The complete text of this important letter was first

[1] "   .   .   .   plus des objurgations et des reproches que des conseils."—Sabatier, Bartholi, p. 120.

[2] *Hist. Seraph.*, fol. 177 v.

[3] Fruct. XXII, P. 11, n. 46. The part here given is that which Wadding exhibits as Epis. VI. M. Sabatier is clearly mistaken in regarding these different abstracts of the letter published separately as so many complete epistles. He says : ".   .   .   Frère Elie ne se corrigeant pas, le saint ne cessa pas de lui faire des recommandations identiques," *l. c.*, p. 119.

[4] See Epis. VIII. This is a different and longer version than that given in the *Conformities*. Wadding gives yet another abstract of the letter as Epis. VII. This he translated from the Spanish, though he confesses misgivings as to the authenticity of its form.

[5] See his edition of Bartholi, pp. 113–131.

[6] See *Frère Elie de Cortone*, p. 51, where the idea of abolishing penances is described as " so Franciscan."

[7] See " The Writings of St. Francis," in the *Month*, January, 1904, pp. 161–164.

published by Fr. Edouard d'Alençon, Archivist General of the Capuchins, in his *Spicilegium Franciscanum*,[1] next by M. Sabatier in his edition of Bartholi,[2] and again by Dr. Lempp in his monograph on Elias.[3] Besides these we have now the versions of Professor Boehmer and the Quaracchi edition. The latter text, which I have here rendered into English, is based on the MSS. of Ognissanti and St. Isidore's (cod. ⅟₂₅) which have been collated with the Neapolitan MS. already referred to and the editions of the letter published by Fr. Edouard d'Alençon and M. Sabatier.

Now for the text of the letter

TO A CERTAIN MINISTER.[4]

To Brother N. . . Minister; may the Lord bless thee.

I speak to thee as best I can on the subject of thy soul; that those things which impede thee

[1] In 1899; after the Vatican MS. 7650, and the Foligno codex. See *Epistola S. Francisci ad ministrum generalem in sua forma authentica cum appendice de Fr. Petro Catanii.*

[2] In 1900, after the Ognissanti MS. See his Bartholi, p. 113.

[3] In 1900. See his *Frère Elie de Cortone*, p. 50 seq.

[4] This is the superscription of the Neapolitan MS. According to the greater number of codices the letter is addressed: "To Brother N . . . Minister." The MSS. of Foligno and St. Isidore's read: "To Brother N . . . Minister General," and some Italian versions cited by M. Sabatier (see Bartholi, p. 121, note 1) add the name of Brother Elias (see also Rodolfo, *l. c.*, fol. 177 v.). The rubric in the second family of MSS. already described (See Introd.) reads simply "Letter which St. Francis sent to the Minister General as to the way to be followed regarding brother subjects sinning mortally or venially." Wadding (*Opusc.*, p. 25, n. 1) thinks the letter was addressed to Peter of Catana. See *Speculum Minorum*, fol. 218 v.

in loving the Lord God and whosoever may be a hindrance to thee, whether brothers or others, even though they were to strike thee,—all these things thou oughtest to reckon as a favor.   And so thou shouldst desire and not otherwise.   And let this be to thee for true obedience from the Lord God and from me; for this I know surely to be true obedience.   And love those that do such things to thee and wish not other from them, save in so far as the Lord may grant to thee ; and in this thing love them,—by wishing that they may be better Christians.[1]   And let this be to thee more than a hermitage.[2]   And by this I wish to know if thou lovest God and me His servant and thine, to wit : that there be no brother in the world who has sinned, how great soever his sin may be, who after he has seen thy face shall ever go away without thy mercy, if he seek mercy,[3] and, if he seek not mercy, ask

---

[1] For the rendering of this doubtful passage : *et in hoc dilige eos ut velis quod sint meliores Christiani*, I have translated the Latin text as given in the Isidorean MS. ⅛₅, in the *Conformities* (fol. 132, v), in Wadding's edition (Epis. VIII), and in that of Quaracchi (p. 108).   In the Ognissanti MS., however, this passage reads *et non velis* "and do *not* desire that they be better Christians."   This reading has been followed by Fr. Edouard d'Alençon and M. Sabatier.   The latter thinks St. Francis is here referring to ungrateful and recalcitrant lepers whom he was wont to call Christians.   But in that hypothesis the passage might be translated "and do not desire to make them better lepers !"

[2] Cod. O. for *eremitorium* reads *meritorium*.   But may not this very improbable reading be that most common thing in early MSS.,—the slip of a copyist ?

[3] Cod. O. omits the remainder of this sentence.

thou him if he desires mercy. And if he afterwards appears [1] before thy face a thousand times,
love him more than me, to the end that thou
mayest draw him to the Lord, and on such ones
always have mercy. And this thou shouldst
declare to the guardians, when thou canst, that
thou art determined of thyself to do thus.

Concerning all the chapters that are in the
Rule that speak of mortal sins [2] we shall at the
chapter of Whitsuntide, God helping, with the
counsel of the brothers, make such a chapter as
this: If any brother, at the instigation of the
enemy, sin mortally, let him be bound by obedience to have recourse to his guardian. And
let all the brothers who know him to have sinned, not cause him shame or slander him, but
let them have great mercy on him and keep very
secret the sin of their brother, for they that are
healthy need not a physician, but they that are
ill.[3] And let them be likewise bound by obedience to send him to his custos with a companion. And let the custos himself care for him
mercifully as he himself would wish to be cared
for by others if he were in a like situation.

[And if he should fall into any [4] venial sin, let
him confess to his brother priest, and if there
be no priest there let him confess to his brother,
until he shall find a priest who shall absolve him

[1] The Neapolitan MS. for "appears" reads "sins."
[2] Chaps. V, XIII, and XX of the first Rule. (See above,
pp. 37, 47, and 53.)
[3] See Matt. 9: 12.
[4] Cod. O. reads: "another."

canonically, as has been said,]¹ and let them have absolutely no power of enjoining other penance save only this : go and sin no more.²

In order that this writing may be able to be better observed, have it by thee until Whitsuntide : thou wilt be there with thy brothers. And these and all other things which are less in the Rule, thou shalt, the Lord God helping, take care to fulfil.

¹ In chap. XX of the First Rule (see above, p. 53). The passage enclosed in brackets is the part omitted by Wadding and those who have followed him.

² See John 8 : 11.

IV.
TO THE RULERS OF THE PEOPLE.

This letter is known to us only by the testimony of the Ven. Francis Gonzaga, O.F.M.,[1] who, speaking of the Province of Aragon in his work on the origin of the Seraphic Order,[2] mentions that Bl. John Parenti, first Minister General after St. Francis (1227—1232), brought a copy of the letter into Spain. On the good faith of Gonzaga, Wadding included this letter in his edition of the *Opuscula*, where it figures as Epist. XV. As the style of the letter and the ideas it embodies corresponded so admirably with the writings of St. Francis, the Quaracchi editors and Professor Goetz,[3] have not hesitated to accept it as genuine. No copy of the letter other than that transcribed by Wadding has so far been found, and it is according to his text of 1623 that it is here translated :—

TO THE RULERS OF THE PEOPLE.

To all *podestàs*, and consuls, judges and governors, in whatever part of the world, and to all others to whom this letter may come, Brother Francis, your little and contemptible servant, wishes health and peace to you.

Consider and see that the day of death draws nigh.[4] I ask you, therefore, with such reverence as I can, not to forget the Lord on account of the cares and solicitudes of this world and not to

---

[1] Minister General of the Order, 1579-1587, afterwards Bishop of Mantua (see *Acta Ordinis Minorum*, 1904, p. 265).

[2] *De Origine Seraphicae Religionis Franciscanae* (Venice 1603), p. 806.

[3] See *Quellen*, etc., p. 535.   [4] See Gen. 47 : 39.

turn aside from His commandments, for all those who forget Him and decline from His commandments are cursed[1] and they shall be forgotten by Him.[2] And when the day of death comes, all that which they think they have shall be taken away from them.[3] And the wiser and more powerful they may have been in this world, so much the greater torments shall they endure in hell.[4]

Wherefore, I strongly advise you, my lords, to put aside all care and solicitude and to receive readily the most holy Body and Blood of our Lord Jesus Christ in holy commemoration of Him. And cause so great honor to be rendered the Lord by the people committed to you, that every evening it may be announced by a crier or by another sign to the end that praises and thanks shall resound to the Lord God Almighty from all the people. And if you do not do this, know that you are beholden to render an account before your Lord God Jesus Christ on the day of Judgment. Let those who keep this writing with them and observe it know that they are blessed by the Lord God.

[1] See Ps. 118 : 21.

[2] See Ezech. 33 : 12.

[3] See Luke 8 : 18.

[4] See Wis. 6 : 7.

V.

To all the Custodes.

Wadding seems to have known of this letter indirectly. At least he gives us a shorter letter addressed to the custodes. The beginning of the epistle he numbers XIV is similar to the one which is translated here and seems to be an incomplete summary of the latter. It is difficult, however, to decide conclusively, since the original form of the letter, which Wadding translated from the Spanish, is wanting. The solution of the question would be to ascertain from what source this Spanish letter was drawn.

The letter was first published in its present form by M. Sabatier in 1900 from a fourteenth century MS. in the Guarnacci library at Volterra.[1] The Quaracchi text is also based on this codex, than which no other version of the letter is known to exist. Internal arguments might, however, be adduced to establish the authenticity of the letter, which is as follows :—

TO ALL THE CUSTODES.

To all the custodes of the Brothers Minor to whom this letter shall come, Brother Francis, your servant and little one in the Lord God, sends greeting with new signs of heaven and earth[2] which on the part of the Lord are great and most excellent and which are accounted least of all by many religious and by other men.

I entreat you more than if it were a question

[1] Cod. 225, mentioned above (p. 110). See Sabatier's Bartholi, p. 135.

[2] Seemingly an allusion to the mysteries of the Eucharist.

of myself that, when it is becoming and it may seem to be expedient, you humbly beseech the clerics to venerate above all the most holy Body and Blood of our Lord Jesus Christ and His Holy Name and written words which sanctify the body.[1] They ought to hold as precious the chalices, corporals, ornaments of the altar, and all that pertain to the Sacrifice. And if the most holy Body of the Lord be lodged very poorly in any place, let It according to the command of the Church be placed by them and left in a precious place, and let It be carried with great veneration and administered to others with discretion. The Names also and written words of the Lord, wheresoever they may be found in unclean places, let them be collected, and they ought to be put in a proper place.

And in all the preaching you do, admonish the people concerning penance and that no one can be saved except he that receives the most sacred Body and Blood of the Lord.[2] And while It is being sacrificed by the priest on the altar and It is being carried to any place, let all the people on bended knees render praise, honor, and glory to the Lord God Living and True.

And you shall so announce and preach His praise to all peoples that at every hour and when the bells are rung praise and thanks shall always be given to the Almighty God by all the people through the whole earth.

---

[1] An obvious reference to the formula of consecration.
[2] See John 6 : 54.

And to whomsoever of my brothers, custodes, this writing shall come, let them copy it and keep it with them and cause it to be copied for the brothers who have the office of preaching and the care of brothers, and let them unto the end preach all those things that are contained in this writing: let them know they have the blessing of the Lord God and mine. And let these be for them through true and holy obedience.

VI.

To Brother Leo.

The authenticity of this letter cannot be challenged. The original autograph is jealously preserved at the Cathedral of Spoleto. In Wadding's time it was kept at the Conventual church in that place, but subsequently disappeared in some way and there was no trace of it until 1895, when Father Cardinali, a priest of Spoleto, placed it in the hands of Mgr. Faloci. The latter presented it to Pope Leo XIII and, after reposing for some three years in the Vatican, it was, at the request of Mgr. Serafini, Archbishop of Spoleto, returned to the cathedral there.[1] Only one other autograph of St. Francis is known to exist.[2] The scope of the letter is obvious : it is a word of tender encouragement and counsel to the *Frate pecorello de Dio*, St. Francis' most intimate companion and friend, who at the time was harassed with doubts and fears. The form of the letter seems to present some difficulties to certain critics. For example, St. Francis at the outset uses the words: *F. Leo F. Francisco tuo salutem et pacem.* It is, of course, clear that this superscription cannot be interpreted in such a way as to make Brother Leo the author of the letter ; in that case it would be *Francisco suo*, and no one, so far as I know, has ever attempted this violence to the text. But there have been some who, thinking St. Francis did not know the difference between a dative and a nomi-

---

[1] See *Gli Autografi di Francesco*, by Mgr. Faloci (*Misc. Franc.*, t. VI, p. 33), and *La Calligrafia di S. Francesco*, by the same author (*Misc. Franc.*, t. VII, p. 67).

[2] The Blessing given to Brother Leo (see below, Part III).

native, have not hesitated to tamper with the text so as to bring the Latin of the *Poverello* into conformity with what they think to be better grammar.[1] I confess that I find no difficulty in translating the superscription as it stands in the original autograph. As a general rule, no doubt, it is the sender of a letter that greets the one to whom it is sent. But, in this case, the humility of St. Francis has led him to change parts and he appeals for a blessing instead of bestowing one. I find myself therefore in thorough accord with Mr. Carmichael's clever solution of this question and agree with him that St. Francis, always imaginative, meant what he wrote, and that "there is really a deep, sweet, and most pathetic meaning in the Saint's peculiar mode of address." Accordingly, the superscription ought to read "Brother Leo, wish thy brother Francis health and peace." It is thus, following Mr. Carmichael, that I have translated it here.

As regards the use of the plural (*faciatis*) in the body of the note which perplexed Wadding, since the singular seems to be called for, some think with the Quaracchi editors that the Saint, writing so familiarly to Leo, adopts the Italian form; others, with M. Sabatier,[2] that Brother Leo had spoken in the name of a group. Perhaps it may not be amiss to recall in this connection, what Celano tells us of St. Francis' method of composition[3] as well as of the letter

---

[1] See, for example, the parallel Latin and Italian text given by Father Bernardo da Fivizzano, O.M.Cap., in his edition of the *Oposculi* (Florence, 1880), which reads: "*F. Leo Frater Franciscus tuus salutem et pacem.*"

[2] "Ce pluriel montre bien que Frère Léon avait parlé au nom d'un groupe."—Sabatier: *Vie de S. François*, p. 301.

[3] When he caused any letters to be written by way of salutation or admonition, he would not suffer any letter or sylla-

of the Saint mentioned by Eccleston, in which
there was faulty Latin.[1] A French critic[2] thinks we
might perhaps be justified in identifying the letter
referred to by Eccleston with the one to Brother Leo
now under consideration. Be this as it may, the
context of the present letter leads one to suppose
that at the time it was written Brother Leo was not
yet habitually with St. Francis. In this hypothesis,
we must fix the date of its composition not later than
1220.[3] It need not be wondered at if, after nearly
seven centuries, some words in the autograph letter
preserved at Spoleto are difficult to read. Hence
some trifling variants occur in the texts published by
Wadding[4] and Faloci.[5] The Quaracchi text which
I have here translated is edited after the original :—

TO BROTHER LEO.

Brother Leo, wish thy brother Francis health
and peace!

I say to thee : Yes, my son, and as a mother ;
for in this word and counsel I sum up briefly all
the words we said on the way, and if afterwards
thou hast need to come to me for advice, thus I
advise you : In whatever way it seemeth best to
thee to please the Lord God and to follow His

ble in them to be erased, though they were often superfluous
or unsuitably placed. (See 1 Cel. 82.)

[1] See Eccleston : *De Adventu Minorum in Angliam* (*Mon.
Germ. hist.*, *Scriptores*, t. XXVIII, p. 563), although another
reading is given in the *Anal. Franc.*, t. I, p. 232, and by Fr.
Cuthbert, O.S.F.C., *The Friars*, etc., p. 167.

[2] Fr. Ubald d'Alençon, *Opuscules*, p. 23.

[3] See *Spec. Perf.* (ed. Sabatier), p. lxiv, note 3.

[4] *Opuscula*, Epist. XVI.

[5] *Misc. Franc.*, t. VI, p. 39.

footsteps and poverty, so do with the blessing of
the Lord God and in my obedience. And if it
be necessary for thee on account of thy soul
or other consolation and thou wishest, Leo, to
come to me, come![1]

[1] It is interesting to compare with this letter the somewhat
similar expressions of encouragement used by St. Francis to
Brother Richer. See 1 Cel. 1, 49; *Spec. Perf.* (ed. Sabatier),
c. 2 and 16; *Actus B. Francisci*, c. 36 and 37.

PART III

PRAYERS OF ST. FRANCIS

I.

THE PRAISES.

THIS opuscule is composed of two parts : a paraphrase of the Lord's Prayer and the Praises properly so-called. It is contained in all the early MS. collections of St. Francis' works[1] either in its entirety as it is given here, or in part—that is, the Paraphrase without the Praises or *vice versa*. With the exception of a single codex which attributes the paternity of this paraphrase to the Blessed Brother Giles,[2] the third companion of St. Francis, the MSS. authorities are unanimous in ascribing the entire work to St. Francis. This fact, taken in conjunction with the internal argument in its favor, puts the authority of the Praises beyond doubt, in the opinion of the Quaracchi editors. M. Sabatier is of like mind and even expresses regret[3] that Professor Boehmer[4] should have been

[1] It is found in the Assisi MS. 338 and in the compilation beginning *Fac secundum exemplar* contained in the Berlin, Lemberg, Liegnitz MSS. and the Vatican codex 4354, as well as in the other family of MSS. represented by the Ognissanti and Foligno MSS. and the codices of St. Isidore's (½₂₅) and the Vatican 7650.

[2] A fourteenth century codex at St. Isidore's Rome (MS. ½₃, fol. 10 v). But I have not found it in any of the collections of Brother Giles' *Dicta* which I have had occasion to consult in preparing the new English version of the same I hope soon to publish.

[3] See *Opuscules*, fasc. x, pp. 136–137. As a postscript to his Examen M. Sabatier gives the text of the paraphrase of the *Our Father* after the rare edition of the *Speculum* (Morin).

[4] See *Analekten*, p. 71.

misled into classing the Praises as doubtful or unau-
thentic. Those who accept the French critic's views
as to the value of his *Speculum Perfectionis* will find
in that remarkable work an additional argument in
favor of the genuinity of the complete opuscule now
engaging our attention. In particular M. Sabatier
applies to the present Praises what is said in the
Speculum of the penance imposed by St. Francis on
the brothers at Portiuncula for speaking idle words.[1]

The Quaracchi Fathers have edited the text of the
Praises according to the Assisian, Antonian, and
Isidorean (¹⁄₂₅) MSS. and have collated these early
versions with the editions of the Praises given in the
Monumenta (fol. 275 v), *Firmamenta* (fol. 18 v), and
the *Liber Conformitatum* (fruct. xii, P. II, c.vi).[2] The
result of their labors is here translated as follows :—

[1] " He also ordained and ordered it to be strictly observed
that any friar who either when doing nothing or at work with
the others, uttered idle words, shall say one *Our Father*,
praising God at the beginning and end of the prayer ; and if
conscious of his fault he accuse himself, he shall say the one
Our Father and the Praises of the Lord for his own soul.
. . . And if on reliable testimony he is shown to have used
idle words, he shall repeat the Praises of the Lord at the beginning and at the end aloud so as to be heard and understood by the surrounding friars," etc. Further on we read :
" The *Praises of the Lord* the most Blessed Father always
said himself, and with ardent desire taught and impressed
upon the friars that they should carefully and devotedly say
the same." See *Spec. Perf.* (ed. Sabatier), c. 82. I have
quoted this passage from Lady de la Warr's translation, pp.
121–122. See also *Opuscules*, fasc. x, p. 137, where M. Sabatier,
speaking of the relation of the *Speculum* to the Praises, says :
" Les deux documents se correspondent, se corroborent et se
garantissent l'un l'autre."

[2] *The Conformities*, edition of 1510, gives the complete text
as the handiwork of St. Francis.

PRAISES.

Here are begun the Praises which the most blessed Father Francis composed; and he said them at all the Hours of the day and night and before the Office of the Blessed Virgin Mary, beginning thus: "Our Father, most holy, who art in heaven," etc., with "Glory be to the Father." Then the Praises, Holy, Holy, etc., are to be said.[1]

Our Father, most holy, our Creator, Redeemer, and Comforter.

Who art in heaven, in the angels and in the saints illuminating them unto knowledge, for Thou, O Lord, art light; inflaming them unto love, for Thou, O Lord, art Love; dwelling in them and filling them with blessedness, for Thou, O Lord, art the highest Good, the eternal Good from whom is all good and without whom is no good.

Hallowed be Thy Name: may Thy knowledge shine in us that we may know the breadth of Thy benefits, the length of Thy promises, the height of Thy majesty, and the depth of Thy judgments.[2]

Thy Kingdom come, that Thou mayest reign in us by grace and mayest make us come to Thy Kingdom, where there is the clear vision of Thee,

[1] Such is the rubric which precedes the Praises in the Assisian MS.

[2] See Eph. 3 : 18.

the perfect love of Thee, the blessed company
of Thee, the eternal enjoyment of Thee.

Thy will be done on earth as it is in heaven, that
we may love Thee with the whole heart by always thinking of Thee; with the whole soul by
always desiring Thee; with the whole mind by
directing all our intentions to Thee and seeking
Thy honor in all things and with all our strength,
by spending all the powers and senses of body
and soul in the service of Thy love and not in
anything else; and that we may love our neighbors even as ourselves, drawing to the best of
our power all to Thy love; rejoicing in the good
of others as in our own and compassionating
[them] in troubles and giving offence to no one.

Give us this day, through memory and understanding and reverence for the love which He
had for us and for those things which He said,
did, and suffered, for us,—*our daily bread*, Thy
Beloved Son, our Lord Jesus Christ.

And forgive us our trespasses, by Thy ineffable
mercy in virtue of the Passion of Thy Beloved
Son, our Lord Jesus Christ, and through the
merits and intercession of the most Blessed
Virgin Mary and of all Thy elect.

As we forgive them that trespass against us,
and what we do not fully forgive, do Thou, O
Lord, make us fully forgive, that for Thy sake
we may truly love our enemies and devoutly
intercede for them with Thee; that we may
render no evil for evil, but in Thee may strive
to do good to all.

And lead us not into temptation, hidden or visible, sudden or continuous.

But deliver us from evil, past, present, and to come. Amen.

Glory be to the Father, etc.

Holy, Holy, Holy, Lord God Almighty, who is and who was and who is to come.[1] Let us praise and exalt Him above all forever.[2]

Worthy art Thou, O Lord, our God, to receive praise, glory and honor and benediction.[3] Let us praise and exalt Him above all forever.

The Lamb that was slain is worthy to receive power and divinity and wisdom and strength and honor and benediction.[4] Let us praise and exalt Him above all forever.

Let us bless the Father and the Son with the Holy Ghost. Let us praise and exalt Him above all forever.

All ye works of the Lord, bless ye the Lord.[5] Let us praise and exalt Him above all forever.

Give praise to God all ye His servants and you that fear Him, little and great.[6] Let us praise and exalt Him above all forever.

Let the heavens and the earth praise Him, the Glorious, and every creature which is in heaven and on earth and under the earth, in the seas and all that are in them.[7] Let us praise and exalt Him above all forever.

[1] See Apoc. 4 : 8.
[2] See Dan. 3 : 57.
[3] See Apoc. 4 : 11.
[4] See Apoc. 5 : 12.
[5] See Dan. 3 : 57.
[6] See Apoc. 19 : 5
[7] See Apoc. 5 : 13.

Glory be to the Father, and to the Son, and to the Holy Ghost. Let us praise and exalt Him above all forever.

As it was in the beginning, is now and ever shall be world without end. Amen. Let us praise and exalt Him above all forever.

Prayer.

Almighty, most holy, most high, and supreme God, highest good, all good, wholly good, who alone art good. To Thee we render all praise, all glory, all thanks, all honor, all blessing, and we shall always refer all good to Thee. Amen.

II.

SALUTATION OF THE BLESSED VIRGIN.

This little prayer enjoys the same title to authenticity as the preceding opuscule, and Professor Boehmer[1] and M. Sabatier[2] are in complete accord with the Quaracchi editors as to its genuinity. With the exception of the Assisi codex, it is found in all the early MS. collections containing the Praises. The text here translated is based on the MS. at Ognissanti and St. Isidore's (½₈), which were collated by the Quaracchi editors with the versions given in the *Conformities* (fruct. xii, P. 11, c. v.) and the *Speculum B. Francisci* (ed. 1 and 2, fol. 127 r).

SALUTATION OF THE BLESSED VIRGIN.[3]

Hail, holy Lady, most holy Queen, Mother of God, Mary who art ever Virgin, chosen from Heaven by the most Holy Father, whom He has consecrated with the most holy beloved Son and the Ghostly Paraclete, in whom was and is all the fulness of grace and all good. Hail thou His palace![4] Hail thou His tabernacle.![5] Hail thou His house. Hail thou His garment! Hail thou His handmaid! Hail thou His Mother and all ye holy virtues which by the grace and

---

[1] *Analekten*, p. xxvii.   [2] *Opuscules*, fasc. x, p. 134.

[3] The text given by Wadding (*Opusc.*, p. 105) was copied by him from an Irish MS. at Salamanca.

[4] Cod. Is. omits from "Hail thou His tabernacle" to "Hail thou His handmaid," inclusive.

[5] Wadding omits from "Hail thou His house" to "Hail thou His handmaid," inclusive.

illumination of the Holy Ghost thou infusest in the heart of the faithful, that from infidels ye mayest make them faithful to God.[1]

[3] The text of the *Conformities* and Wadding here add the second part of the antiphon given below in the Office of the Passion beginning "Mother of our most Holy Lord Jesus Christ," etc.   In the *Speculum* (ed. Morin, 1509) this Salutation is followed by another prayer to the Blessed Virgin (see Sabatier, *Opuscules*, fasc. x, p. 164); but from the beginning of the seventeenth century, the second prayer is no longer found in the text of the *Speculum* (see the edition of Spoelberch, P. I, pp. 176–178, and Wadding, *Opusc.*, p. 107). In the opinion of Professor Boehmer this Salutation ought to follow immediately after the Salutation of the Virtues given above (p. 20).   See his *Analekten*, pp. vi and xxviii.   They are found in this order in the *Spec. Vitae* of 1504 and the Vatican MS. 4354.

III.

Prayer to Obtain Divine Love.

The authenticity of this prayer, accepted by the Quaracchi editors, rests on the authority of St. Bernardine of Siena[1] and Ubertino da Casale,[2] both of whom are quoted in its behalf by Wadding. The prayer is here translated according to the text given by Ubertino in his *Arbor Vitae Crucifixae* composed on La Verna in 1305.[3] It follows :—

PRAYER.

I beseech Thee, O Lord, that the fiery and sweet strength of Thy love may absorb my soul from all things that are under heaven, that I may die for love of Thy love as Thou didst deign to die for love of my love.

---

[1] St. Bernardine died in 1444. See his *Opera Omnia*, t. II, sermo 60, art. 11, c. 11.

[2] See *Arbor Vitae*, l. v, c. iv.

[3] See Ehrle, *Archiv*, etc., vol. II, pp. 374-416, as to the writings of Ubertino.

IV.

The Sheet which St. Francis gave Brother Leo.

The earliest witness to this document is Thomas of Celano, who in his Second Life (written about 1247) records that "while the Saint was remaining secluded in his cell on Mount La Verna, one of the companions conceived a great desire to have some memorial from words of the Lord written by the hand of St. Francis and briefly annotated by him. .   One day Blessed Francis called him, saying, 'Bring me paper and ink, for I wish to write the words of God and His praises which I have been meditating in my heart.' What he asked for being straightway brought, he writes with his own hand the praises of God and the words which he [his companion] wished, and lastly a blessing of the brother, saying : 'Take this sheet (*chartulam*) for thyself and until the day of thy death guard it carefully.' All temptation was at once driven away ; the letter is kept and worked wonders for the time to come."[1]

The original autograph of the sheet here described by Celano is reverently preserved in the sacristy of the Sacro Convento at Assisi.[2] It has been mentioned in the archives of the convent since 1348 and is borne in procession annually at the opening of the feast of the "Perdono" or Portiuncula Indulgence. Many pages have been consecrated by scholars[3] to

[1] 2 Cel. 2, 18; see also Bonav. *Leg. Maj.*, XI, 9, where the narration is clearly borrowed from Celano.

[2] A photograph of the reliquary containing it is here reproduced.

[3] For example Papini *La Storia di S. Francesco*, t. I, p. 130, n. 8, Grisar, see *Civilta Cattolica*, fasc. 1098 (1896), p. 723; Mgr. Faloci Pulignani, *Misc. Franc.*, t. VI (1895), p. 34; Fr.

this small, crumpled piece of parchment and as they are easily accessible it would be superfluous to touch here upon the controversial *minutiae* connected with it. Suffice it to say that on the reverse side of the sheet containing the Praises is found the Biblical blessing. The latter was dictated to Brother Leo, but at the bottom St. Francis himself wrote the personal blessing, adding what Wadding described as a "large and mysterious *thau* or letter *T*'' which he was wont to use as his signature, as both Celano[1] and St. Bonaventure[2] inform us.

To authenticate this relic Brother Leo himself added to it three notes; the first reads: "Blessed Francis wrote with his own hand this blessing for me, Brother Leo;'' and the second: "In like manner he made this sign *thau* together with the head with his own hand." More valuable still is the third annotation, since it fixes the date of this precious document. I give it in full: "Blessed Francis two years before his death kept a Lent in the place of Mount La Verna in honor of the Blessed Virgin Mary, the Mother of the Lord, and of the blessed Michael the Archangel, from the feast of the Assumption of the

Edouard d'Alençon, *La Benediction de St. François;* M. Sabatier, *Spec. Perf.*, pp. lxvii–lxx; Reginald Balfour, *The Seraphic Keepsake;* and Montgomery Carmichael, *La Benedizione di San Francesco.* See also Fr. Saturnino da Caprese, O.F.M., *Guida Illustrata della Verna* (Prato, 1902), p. 93. On the testimony of three leading German palæographers, Wattenbach, Dziatzko and Meyer, see *Theol. Literatur-Zeitung*, Leipzig, 1895, pp. 404 and 627.

[1] Says Celano: "The sign *thau* was more familiar to him than other signs. With it only he signed sheets for despatch and he painted it on the walls of the cells anywhere." See *Tr. de Miraculis*, in *Anal. Boll.*, t. xviii, pp. 114–115.

[2] "He signed it upon all the letters he directed." See Bonav. *Leg. Maj.*, IV, 3.

holy Virgin Mary until the September feast- of St. Michael. And the hand of the Lord was laid upon him; after the vision and speech of the Seraph and the impression of the Stigmata of Christ in his body he made and wrote with his own hand the Praises written on the other side of the sheet, giving thanks to the Lord for the benefits conferred on him.''

An examination of the original autograph shows that, while the side of the sheet containing the Blessing is excellently preserved, the other one on which the Praises are written, is, for the most part, illegible and in consequence some variants are to be found in different MS. versions of it. After a careful collation of these MSS. with the autograph, the Quaracchi editors found the Assisi codex 344 more conformable to the original than any other. It is after this fourteenth century MS. of the library of the Sacro Convento and which appears to have been copied from the autograph, that the Quaracchi editors published the text which I now translate :—

PRAISES OF GOD.

Thou art holy, Lord God, who alone workest wonders. Thou art strong. Thou art great. Thou art most high. Thou art the Almighty King, Thou, holy Father, King of heaven and earth. Thou art the Lord God Triune and One; all good. Thou art good, all good, highest good, Lord God living and true. Thou art charity, love.[1] Thou art wisdom. Thou art humility. Thou art patience. Thou art security. Thou art quietude. Thou art joy and gladness. Thou

---

[1] These words seem to be transposed in the autograph.

art justice and temperance. Thou art all riches to sufficiency.[1] Thou art beauty. Thou art meekness. Thou art protector. Thou art guardian and defender. Thou art strength. Thou art refreshment. Thou art our hope. Thou art our faith. Thou art our great sweetness. Thou art our eternal life, great and admirable Lord, God Almighty, merciful Saviour.

After this expression of the mystical ardors which consumed the *Poverello* comes :—

THE BLESSING OF BROTHER LEO.

May the Lord bless thee and keep thee. May He shew His face to thee and have mercy on thee. May He turn His countenance to thee and give thee peace.[2] Brother LeTo[3] may the Lord bless thee.

[1] From this point to the end of the Praises the autograph is illegible.

[2] See Num. 6 : 24–26.

[3] Mr. Balfour points out that the position of Leo's name in relation to the *thau* is intentional and that the *thau* thus becomes a cross of blessing, St. Francis, following the practice of all old Missals and Breviaries, having placed it so as to divide the name of the person blessed. See *The Seraphic Keepsake*, p. 106.

V.

THE CANTICLE OF THE SUN.

Of the several "cantica in vulgari" which St. Francis composed, the only one that has come down to us, as far as is known, is the "Praises of the Creatures," or, as it is now more commonly called, "The Canticle of the Sun." Celano, who alludes to this laud, says of St. Francis that he was of the race of Ananias, Azarias and Misael, inviting all creatures with him to glorify Him who made them.[1] It is this side of St. Francis' thoughts which finds expression in the Canticle; and in this particular order of ideas modern religious poetry has never produced anything comparable to this sublime improvisation into which have passed alike "all the wealth of the Saint's imagination and all the boldness of his genius." [2] Tradition tells us that Fra Pacifico had a hand in the embellishment of this laud,[3] about which a whole controversial literature has grown.[4] Some light may perhaps be thrown on this delicate question in the new critical edition of the Canticle promised by Luigi Suttina.

The Canticle appears to have been composed toward the close of the year 1225 in a poor little hut near the Monastery of San Damiano, whither St.

[1] See 2 Cel. 3, 138–139, and 1 Cel. 80.

[2] See Cherancé, *Life of St. Francis*, p. 260.

[3] See on this head Ozanam, *Les Poètes Franciscains*, p. 82, and Matthew Arnold, *Essays on Criticism*, pp. 243–248. Mr. Arnold's translation of the Canticle is well known.

[4] For a list of the more important studies on it, see *Speculum Perfectionis* (ed. Sabatier), p. 289; L. Suttina, *Appunti bibliografici di studi francescani*, p. 19; also Gasparry's *Italian Literature to the death of Dante*, p. 358.

Francis had retired on account of his infirmities, and, if we may believe the tradition which finds formal expression in the *Speculum Perfectionis*, two strophes were subsequently added by the Saint to the original composition, — the eighth strophe upon the occasion of a feud between the Bishop and the magistrates of Assisi, and the ninth one when the Saint recognized the approach of death. M. Renan, with what Canon Knox Little[1] calls "his characteristic inaccuracy," asserts that we do not possess the Italian original of the Canticle, but have only an Italian translation from the Portuguese, which was in turn translated from the Spanish.[2] And yet the original Italian text exists, as M. Sabatier notes,[3] not only in numerous MSS. in Italy and France, notably in the Assisi MS. 338[4] and at the Mazarin Library,[5] but also in the *Book of the Conformities*.

The Canticle is accepted as authentic by Professors Boehmer and Goetz in their recent works on the *Opuscula* of St. Francis. If it does not figure in the Quaracchi edition, the reason is that the *Bibliotheca Franciscana Ascetica Medii Ævi*, of which the *Opuscula* forms part, is confined to works written in Latin, and hence M. Sabatier's animadversions on the "theological preoccupations" of the Quaracchi editors are altogether aside the mark.

The text of the Canticle here translated is that of the Assisi MS. 338 (fol. 33), from which the version

---

[1] See his *St. Francis of Assisi*, p. 235, note 2.

[2] See *Nouvelles Etudes d'histoire religieuse*, p. 331.

[3] *Vie de S. François*, p. xxxiv and chap. xviii.

[4] This text was published by Fr. Panfilo da Magliano, O.F.M., in his *Storia Compendiosa*, also by M. Sabatier in his *Vie de S. François* and later in his *Speculum*, pp. 334-35.

[5] Professor Boehmer published the text of the Maz. MS. 1350 in his *Sonnengesang v. Fr. d'A.*, in 1871.

given in the *Conformities* (pars. 2, fol. ii)[1] differs only
by some unimportant variants. The following is an
attempt to render literally into English the naïf
rhythm of the original Italian, which necessarily dis-
appears in any formal rhymed translation :

HERE BEGIN THE PRAISES OF THE CREATURES
WHICH THE BLESSED FRANCIS MADE TO THE
PRAISE AND HONOR OF GOD WHILE HE WAS ILL
AT ST. DAMIAN'S :

Most high, omnipotent, good Lord,
Praise, glory and honor and benediction
    all, are Thine.
To Thee alone do they belong, most High,
And there is no man fit to mention Thee.

Praise be to Thee, my Lord, with all Thy crea-
    tures,
Especially to my worshipful brother sun,
The which lights up the day, and through him
    dost Thou brightness give ;
And beautiful is he and radiant with splendor
    great ;

Of Thee, most High, signification gives.

Praised be my Lord, for sister moon and for the
    stars,
In heaven Thou hast formed them clear and
    precious and fair.

---

[1] I have had the advantage of studying two of the oldest
MSS. of this work known,—those of the convents of La Verna
and Portiuncula.

Praised be my Lord for brother wind
And for the air and clouds and fair and every
    kind of weather,
By the which Thou givest to Thy creatures
    nourishment.
Praised be my Lord for sister water,
The which is greatly helpful and humble and
    precious and pure.

Praised be my Lord for brother fire,
By the which Thou lightest up the dark.
And fair is he and gay and mighty and strong.

Praised be my Lord for our sister, mother earth,
The which sustains and keeps us
And brings forth diverse fruits with grass and
    flowers bright.

Praised be my Lord for those who for Thy love
    forgive
And weakness bear and tribulation.
Blessed those who shall in peace endure,
For by Thee, most High, shall they be crowned.

Praised be my Lord for our sister, the bodily
    death,
From the which no living man can flee.
Woe to them who die in mortal sin ;
Blessed those who shall find themselves in Thy
    most holy will,
For the second death shall do them no ill.

Praise ye and bless ye my Lord, and give Him
    thanks,
And be subject unto Him with great humility.

VI.

The Office of the Passion.

Although the early biographies of St. Francis are silent as to this opuscule, its authenticity is guaranteed by the Legend of St. Clare written by Thomas of Celano toward the end of his life.[1]   In reference to the holy abbess' devotion to the Passion we are told by Celano that she "learned and frequently recited with attachment the Office of the Cross which Francis, the lover of the Cross, had instituted."[2] This passage was rightly understood by Wadding as referring to the Office of the Passion which many early MSS. attribute to St. Francis, and the character of which altogether squares with the Saint's writings.   Composed, as it is, of a simple and devout combination of Scriptural texts, this document is at once a witness to St. Francis' ardent devotion to the Crucified and a precious example of his method of prayer.   It comprises five parts :

1. For the three last days of Holy Week and for week-days throughout the year.

2. For the Paschal season.

3. For Sundays and feast-days throughout the year.

4. For Advent.

5. For Christmas and the days following, to the close of the Epiphany octave.

The text of the Office given in the Quaracchi edition is that of the Assisi MS. 338, only a few rubrical notes having been omitted.   The Office may also be

---

[1] It was soon after the canonization of St. Clare, about 1256, that Celano undertook the task of compiling this legend by order of Alexander IV.

[2] See *Acta S.S.*, t. II, Aug., p. 761.

found in MSS. at Oxford,[1] Berlin,[2] and Liegnitz[3] already described.[4] It has never before, so far as I know, been translated into English. Here it is :—

OFFICE OF THE PASSION OF THE LORD.

Here begin the Psalms which our most blessed Father Francis arranged to reverence and recall and praise the Passion of the Lord. And they begin from Compline on Maundy Thursday because on that night our Lord Jesus Christ was betrayed and taken captive. And note that the Blessed Francis was wont to say this office thus : First he said the Prayer which the Lord and Master taught us : *Our Father most holy*,[5] with the Praises, to wit, *Holy, Holy, Holy*.[6] When he had finished the Praises with the Prayer he began this antiphon, namely : *Holy Mary*. First he said the Psalms of the holy Virgin ; besides he said other Psalms which he had selected, and at the end of all the Psalms which he said, he said the Psalms of the Passion, the Psalm being finished he said the antiphon, namely, *Holy Virgin Mary*. When this antiphon was finished, the office was completed.

I.—AT COMPLINE.

Ant. Holy Virgin Mary.

Psalm.

Ps. 55 : 9. O God, I have declared to Thee my life ; Thou hast set my tears in Thy sight.

[1] See Little in *Opuscules*, t. I, p. 276.

[2] See *Spec. Perf.* (ed. Sabatier), p. cxcvi.

[3] See *Opuscules*, t. I, p. 55. This MS. contains only the first part of the Office ; it ends with the words the "Lord hath reigned."

[4] See above, p. 3-4. Other MSS. containing the Office are enumerated by Wadding. See also Boehmer's *Analekten*.

[5] See above, p. 139.

[6] See above, p. 141.

Ps. 40 : 8. All my enemies devised evils against me.

Ps. 70 : 10. They have consulted together.

Ps. 108 : 5. And they have repaid me evil for good and hatred for my love.

Ps. 108 : 4. Instead of making me a return of love they detracted me; but I gave myself to prayer.

Ps. 21 : 12. My holy Father, King of heaven and earth, depart not from me; for tribulation is near and there is none to help.

Ps. 55 : 10. When I cry unto Thee, then shall mine enemies be turned back; behold I know that thou art my God.

Ps. 37 : 12. My friends and my neighbors have drawn near and stood against me; and they that were near me stood afar off.

Ps. 87 : 9. Thou hast put away my acquaintance far from me; they have set me an abomination to them; I was delivered up and came not forth.

Ps. 21 : 20. Holy Father, remove not Thy help far from me: My God, look toward my help.

Ps. 37 : 23. Attend unto my help, O Lord, the God of my salvation,—Glory be.
Holy Virgin Mary, there is none like unto Thee born in the world among women, daughter and hand-

maid of the most high King, the heavenly Father! Mother of our most holy Lord Jesus Christ, Spouse of the Holy Ghost; pray for us, with St. Michael Archangel, and all the Virtues of heaven, and all the Saints, to thy most holy, beloved Son, our Lord and Master. Glory be to the Father and to the Son and to the Holy Ghost. As it was in the beginning is now and ever shall be world without end. Amen.

Note that the foregoing antiphon is said at all the Hours and it is said for antiphon, chapter, hymn, versicle, and prayer, and at Matins and at all the Hours likewise. He said nothing else in them except this antiphon with its Psalms. At the completion of the office Blessed Francis always said: Let us bless the Lord God living and true; let us refer praise, glory, honor, blessing and all praise to Him, always. Amen. Amen. Fiat. Fiat.

AT MATINS.

Ant. Holy Virgin Mary.

Psalm.

Ps. 87: 2. O Lord, the God of my salvation, I have cried in the day and night before Thee.

Ps. 87: 3. Let my prayer come in before Thee; incline Thy ear to my petition.

Ps. 68: 19. Attend to my soul and deliver it: save me because of my enemies.

Ps. 21 : 10. For Thou art He that hast drawn me out of the womb; my hope from the breasts of my mother;

Ps. 21 : 11. I was cast upon Thee from the womb. From my mother's womb Thou art my God;

Ps. 21 : 12. Depart not from me.

Ps. 68 : 20. Thou knowest my reproach and my confusion and my shame.

Ps. 68 : 21. In Thy sight are all they that afflict me: my heart hath expected reproach and misery.

And I looked for one that would grieve together with me, but there was none, and for one that would comfort me and I found none.

Ps. 85 : 14. O God, the wicked are risen up against me and the assembly of the mighty have sought my soul; and they have not set Thee before their eyes.

Ps. 87 : 5. I am counted among them that go down to the pit; I am become as a man without help,

Ps. 87 : 6. free among the dead.

Thou art my Father, most holy, my king and my God.

Ps. 37 : 23. Attend unto my help, O Lord God of my salvation.

Ant. Holy Mary.

Psalm.

Ps. 56: 1. Have mercy on me, O God, have mercy on me; for my soul trusteth in Thee.

Ps. 56: 2. And in the shadow of Thy wings will I hope, until iniquity pass away.

Ps. 56: 3. I will cry to my most holy Father, the Most High: to God, who hath done good to me;

Ps. 56: 4. He hath sent from heaven and delivered me; He hath made them a reproach that trod upon me.
God hath sent His power and His truth.

Ps. 17: 18. He delivered me from my strongest enemies and from them that hated me; for they were too strong for me.

Ps. 56: 7. They prepared a snare for my feet; and they bowed down my soul; they dug a pit before my face; and they are fallen into it.

Ps. 56: 8. My heart is ready, O God, my heart is ready; I will sing, and rehearse a psalm.

Ps. 56: 9. Arise, O my glory, arise psaltery and harp;
I will arise early.

Ps. 56 : 10. I will give praise to Thee, O Lord, among the people; I will sing a psalm to Thee among the nations;

Ps. 56 : 11. For Thy mercy is magnified even to the heavens; and Thy truth unto the clouds.

Ps. 56 : 12. Be Thou exalted, O God, above the heavens; and Thy glory above all the earth.

AT TIERCE.

Ant. Holy Mary.

Psalm.

Ps. 55 : 2. Have mercy on me, O God, for man hath trodden me under foot; all the day long he hath afflicted me, fighting against me.

Ps. 55 : 3. My enemies have trodden on me all the day long; for they are many that make war against me.

Ps. 40 : 8. All my enemies devised evil against me;

Ps. 70 : 10. they have taken counsel together.

Ps. 40 : 7. They went out and spoke to the same purpose.

Ps. 21 : 8. All they that saw me have laughed me to scorn; they have spoken with the lips and wagged the head.

Ps. 21 : 7. But I am a worm and no man, a

reproach of men and outcast of the people.

Ps. 30 : 12. I am become a reproach among all my enemies and very much to my neighbors; and a fear to my acquaintance.

Ps. 21 : 20. Holy Father, remove not Thy help far from me; my God, look toward my defense.

Ps. 37 : 23. Attend unto my help, O Lord God of my salvation. Glory be, etc.

AT SEXT.

Ant. Holy Mary.

Psalm.

Ps. 141 : 2. I cried to the Lord, with my voice; with my voice I made my supplication to the Lord.

Ps. 141 : 3. I pour out my prayer in His sight; and before Him I declare my trouble.

Ps. 141 : 4. When my spirit failed me, then Thou knewest my paths. In this way wherein I walked, they have hidden a snare for me.

Ps. 141 : 5. I looked on my right-hand, and beheld, and there was no one that would know me. Flight hath failed me; and there is no one that hath regard to my soul.

Ps. 68 : 8. Because for Thy sake I have borne reproach; shame hath covered my face.

Ps. 68 : 9. I am become a stranger to my brethren; and an alien to the sons of my mother.

Ps. 68 : 10. Holy Father, the zeal of Thy house hath eaten me up; and the reproaches of them that reproached Thee are fallen upon me.

Ps. 34 : 15. And they rejoiced against me and gathered together; scourges were gathered together upon me and I knew not.

Ps. 68 : 5. They are multiplied above the hairs of my head who hate me without cause;
My enemies are grown strong who have wrongfully persecuted me; then did pay I that which I took not away.

Ps. 34 : 11. Unjust witnesses rising up, have asked me things I knew not.

Ps. 34 : 12. They repaid me evil for good and

Ps. 37 : 21. detracted me; because I followed goodness.
Thou art my Father, most holy; my King and my God.

Ps. 37 : 23. Attend unto my help, O Lord God of my salvation.

AT NONES.

Ant. Holy Mary.

Psalm.

Lam. 1 : 12. O all ye that pass by, attend and see if there be any sorrow like to my sorrow.

Ps. 21 : 17. For many dogs have encompassed me; the council of the malignant hath besieged me.

Ps. 21 : 18. They looked and stared upon me;

Ps. 21 : 19. they parted my garments among them and upon my vesture cast lots.

Ps. 21 : 17. They have dug my hands and my feet;

Ps. 21 : 18. they numbered all my bones.

Ps. 21 : 14. They have opened their mouth against me : as a lion ravening and roaring.

Ps. 21 : 15. I am poured out like water and all my bones are scattered.
And my heart is become like melting wax in the midst of my bowels.

Ps. 21 : 16. My strength is dried up like a potsherd ; and my tongue hath cleaved to my jaws.

Ps. 68 : 22. And they gave me gall for my food : and in my thirst they gave me vinegar to drink.

Ps. 21 : 16. And Thou hast brought me into the dust of death ;

Ps. **68** : 27. and they have added to the grief
of my wounds.

I slept and rose again; and my
most holy Father received me with
glory.

Ps. 72 : 24. Holy Father, Thou hast held my
right hand; and by Thy will Thou
hast conducted me and hast received me with glory.

Ps. 72 : 25. For what have I in heaven; and
besides Thee what do I desire
upon earth?

Ps. 45 : 11. Be still and see that I am God,
saith the Lord; I will be exalted
among the nations and I will be
exalted in the earth.

Blessed is the Lord God of Israel,

Ps. 33 : 23. who has redeemed the souls of
His servants with His own most
holy Blood; and none of them that
trust in Him shall offend.

Ps. 95 : 13. And we know that He cometh; for
He will come to judge justice.

AT VESPERS.

Ant. Holy Mary.

Psalm.

Ps. 46 : 2. O clap your hands, all ye nations,
shout unto God with the voice of
joy.

Ps. 46: 3. For the Lord is ·high, terrible:
He is a great king over all the
earth.

For the most holy Father of heaven,
our King, before ages sent His beloved Son from on high:

Ps. 73: 12. and hath wrought salvation in the
midst of the earth.

Ps. 95: 11. Let the heavens rejoice and let the
earth be glad, let the sea be moved
and the fulness thereof:

Ps. 95: 12. the fields and all that are in them
shall be joyful.

Ps. 95: 1. Sing unto Him a new canticle; sing
unto the Lord, all the earth.

Ps. 95: 4. For the Lord is great and exceedingly to be praised;
He is to be feared above all gods.

Ps. 95: 7. Bring to the Lord, O ye kindreds
of the gentiles, bring to the Lord
glory and honor.

Ps. 95: 8. Bring to the Lord glory unto His
Name.

Bring your own bodies and bear
His holy cross; and follow His
most holy precepts even unto the
end.

Ps. 95: 9. Let all the earth be moved at His
presence;

Ps. 95: 10. say among the gentiles that the
Lord hath reigned.

It is said up to this place daily from Good Friday until the feast of the Ascension. On the feast of the Ascension, however, these versicles are added over and above :

> And He ascended unto heaven; and sitteth on the right-hand of the most Holy Father in heaven.

Ps. 56 : 12. Be Thou exalted, O God, above the heavens; and Thy glory above all the earth.

Ps. 95 : 13. And we know that He cometh : for He will come to judge justice.

And note that from the Ascension until the Advent of the Lord this Psalm is said daily in the same manner, namely: "O clap your hands," with the foregoing versicles, "Glory be to the Father" being said where the Psalm ends, namely, "for He will come to judge with justice."

Note that the foregoing Psalms are said from Good Friday until Easter Sunday : they are said in the same manner from the octave of Whitsunday until the Advent of the Lord and from the octave of the Epiphany until Maundy Thursday,[1] except on Sundays, and the principal feasts, on which they are not said : on the other days however they are said daily.

HOLY SATURDAY AT COMPLINE.

Ant. Holy Mary.

Psalm.

Ps. 69 : 2. O God, *etc.* (Ps. 69), *as in the Psalter.*

It is said daily at Compline until the octave of Pentecost.

[1] The Oxford Codex here reads "until Easter Sunday."

EASTER SUNDAY AT MATINS.

Ant. Holy Mary.

Psalm.

Ps. 97: 1. Sing ye to the Lord a new canticle: for He hath done wonderful things. His right hand hath sanctified His Son; and His arm is holy.

Ps. 97: 2. The Lord hath made known His salvation; He hath revealed His justice in the sight of the gentiles.

Ps. 41: 9. In the day time the Lord hath commanded His mercy: and a canticle to Him in the night.

Ps. 117: 24. This is the day which the Lord hath made: let us rejoice and be glad in it.

Ps. 117: 26. Blessed be He that cometh in the name of the Lord.

Ps. 117: 27. The Lord is God and He hath shone upon us.

Ps. 95: 11. Let the heavens rejoice and let the earth be glad: let the sea be moved and the fulness thereof.

Ps. 95: 12. The fields shall rejoice and all that are in them.

Ps. 95: 7. Bring to the Lord, O ye kindreds of the gentiles, bring to the Lord glory and honor:

Ps. 95: 8. bring to the Lord glory unto His Name.

It is said up to this place daily from Easter Sunday to the feast of the Ascension at all the Hours except at Vespers and Compline and Prime. On the night of the Ascension these verses are added :—

Ps. 67 : 33. Sing ye to God, ye kingdoms of the earth : sing ye to the Lord : sing ye to God,

Ps. 67 : 34. who mounteth above the heaven of heavens to the east. Behold He will give to His voice the voice of power :

Ps. 67 : 35. give ye glory to God for Israel : His magnificence and His power is in the clouds.

Ps. 67 : 36. God is wonderful in His saints : the God of Israel is He who will give power and strength to His people. Blessed be God.

And note that this Psalm is said daily from the Ascension of the Lord until the octave of Whitsunday with the foregoing versicles at Matins and Tierce and Sext and Nones : "Glory be to the Father," being said where "Blessed be God " is said, and not elsewhere. Also note that it is said in the same manner only at Matins on Sundays and the principal feasts, from the octave of Whitsunday until Maundy Thursday because on that day the Lord ate the Pasch with His disciples, or the other Psalm may be said at Matins or at Vespers when one wishes, to wit, " I will extol Thee, O Lord," as it is in the Psalter, and this from Easter Sunday to the feast of the Ascension and not longer.

AT PRIME.

Ant. Holy Mary.

Psalm. Have mercy on me, etc.—*as above, p.* 159.

AT TIERCE, SEXT AND NONES.
Psalm. Sing ye to the Lord, etc. —*as above*, p. 167.

AT VESPERS.
Psalm. O clap your hands, etc.—*as above,p.* 164.

Here begin the other psalms which our most blessed Father Francis likewise arranged which are to be said in place of the foregoing psalms of the Passion of the Lord on Sunday and the principal festivities from the octave of Whitsunday until Advent and from the octave of the Epiphany until Maundy Thursday.

AT COMPLINE.
Ant. Holy Mary.
Psalm. O God, etc. (Ps. 69),—*as it is in the Psalter.*

AT MATINS.
Ant. Holy Mary.
Psalm. Sing ye to the Lord, etc.,—*as above,p.* 167.

AT PRIME.
Ant. Holy Mary.
Psalm. Have mercy on me, etc.,—*as above,p.* 159.

AT TIERCE.
Ant. Holy Mary.
Psalm.

Ps. 65 : 1. Shout with joy to God, all the earth.
Ps. 65 : 2. Sing ye a Psalm to His name : give glory to His praise.
Ps. 65 : 3. Say unto God, How terrible are Thy works, O Lord : in the multi-

tude of Thy strength Thy enemies shall lie to Thee.

Ps. 65 : 4. Let all the earth adore Thee and sing to Thee : let it sing a psalm to Thy Name.

Ps. 65 : 16. Come and hear, all ye that fear God, and I will tell you what great things He hath done for my soul.

Ps. 65 : 17. I cried to Him with my mouth : and I extolled Him with my tongue.

Ps. 17 : 7. And He heard my voice from His holy temple : and my cry came before Him.

Ps. 65 : 8. O bless our God, ye gentiles : and make the voice of His praise to be heard.

Ps. 71 : 17. And in him shall all the tribes of the earth be blessed : all nations shall magnify Him.

Ps. 71 : 18. Blessed be the Lord God of Israel, who only doth wonderful things.

Ps. 71 : 19. And blessed be the Name of His majesty forever : and the whole earth shall be filled with His majesty. Amen. Amen.

AT SEXT.

Ant. Holy Mary.

Psalm.

Ps. 19 : 2. May the Lord hear thee in the day of tribulation : may the Name of the God of Jacob protect thee : may He

Ps. 19 : 3. send thee help from the sanctuary and defend thee out of Sion :

Ps. 19 : 4. be mindful of all thy sacrifices, and may thy whole burnt-offering be made fat ;

Ps. 19 : 5. Give thee according to thy own heart, and confirm all thy counsels.

Ps. 19 : 6. We will rejoice in thy salvation ; and in the Name of our God we shall be exalted.

Ps. 19 : 7. The Lord fulfil all thy petitions : now I know that the Lord hath sent Jesus Christ His Son,

Ps. 9 : 9. and will judge the people with justice.

Ps. 9 : 10. And the Lord is become a refuge for the poor : a helper in due time of tribulation.

Ps. 9 : 11. And let them trust in Thee who know Thy Name.

Ps. 143 : 1. Blessed be the Lord my God :

Ps. 58 : 17. for Thou art become my support and refuge in the day of my trouble.

Ps. 58 : 18. Unto Thee, O my helper, will I sing : for God is my defence, my God, my mercy.

AT NONES.

Ant. Holy Mary.

Psalm.

Ps. 70 : 1. In Thee, O Lord, have I hoped, let me never be put to confusion.

Ps. 70 : 2. Deliver me in Thy justice and res-
cue me : incline Thine ear unto
and save me.

Ps. 70 : 3. Be Thou unto me, O God, a protector and a place of strength : that
Thou mayest make me safe.

Ps. 70 : 5. For Thou art my patience, O Lord ;
my hope, O Lord, from my youth.

Ps. 70 : 6. By Thee have I been confirmed
from the womb, from my mother's
womb Thou art my protector : of
Thee I shall continually sing.

Ps. 70 : 8. Let my mouth be filled with praise,
that I may sing Thy glory ; Thy
greatness all the day long.

Ps. 68 : 17. Hear me, O Lord, for Thy mercy is
kind ; look upon me according to the
multitude of Thy tender mercies.

Ps. 68 : 18. And turn not away Thy face from
Thy servant ; for I am in trouble,
hear me speedily.

Ps. 143 : 1. Blessed be the Lord my God.

Ps. 58 : 17. For Thou art become my support
and refuge in the day of my trouble.

Ps. 58 : 18. Unto Thee, O my helper, will I
sing ; for God is my defence, my
God, my mercy.

AT VESPERS.

Ant. Holy Mary.

Psalm. O clap your hands.   . *as above, p.*
164.

Here begin other Psalms which our most blessed Father Francis likewise arranged; which are to be said in place of the foregoing Psalms of the Passion of the Lord from the Advent of the Lord until Christmas eve and not longer.

AT COMPLINE.

Ant. Holy Mary.

Psalm. How long, O Lord (Ps. 12), *as it is found in the Psalter.*

AT MATINS.

Ant. Holy Mary.

Psalm.

Ps. 85 : 12. I will praise Thee, O Lord, most Holy Father, King of heaven and earth; because

Ps. 85 : 17. Thou hast comforted me.

Ps. 24 : 5. Thou art God my Saviour.

Ps. 11 : 6. I will deal confidently and will not fear.

Ps. 117 : 14. The Lord is my strength and my praise; and is become my salvation.

Exod. 15 : 6. Thy right hand, O Lord, is magnified in strength;
Thy right hand, O Lord, hath slain the enemy:

Exod. 15 : 7. And in the multitude of Thy glory Thou hast put down Thy adversaries.

Ps. 68 : 33. Let the poor see and rejoice: seek ye God and your soul shall live.

Ps. 68 : 35. Let the heavens and the earth praise Him : the sea and everything that creepeth therein.

Ps. 68 : 36. For God will save Sion and the cities of Juda shall be built up.
And they shall dwell there : and acquire it by inheritance.

Ps. 68 : 37. And the seed of His servants shall possess it : and they that love His Name shall dwell therein.

AT PRIME.

Ant. Holy Mary.

Psalm. Have mercy on me, etc.—*as above, p.* 159.

AT TIERCE.

Ant. Holy Mary.

Psalm. Shout with joy, etc.—*as above, p.* 169.

AT SEXT.

Ant. Holy Mary.

Psalm. May the Lord hear thee in the day, etc. —*as above, p.* 170.

AT NONES.

Ant. Holy Mary.

Psalm. In Thee, O Lord, have I hoped—*as above, p.* 171.

AT VESPERS.

Ant. Holy Mary.

Psalm. O clap your hands, etc.—*as above, p.* 164.

Also note that the whole Psalm is not said but up to the verse, " Let all the earth be moved "; understand

however that the whole verse " Bring your own bodies "
must be said.   At the end of this verse " Glory be to the
Father " is said.   And thus it is said daily at Vespers
from Advent until Christmas eve.

CHRISTMAS DAY AT VESPERS.

Ant. Holy Mary.

Psalm.

Ps. 80 : 2. Rejoice to God our helper.

Ps. 46 : 2. Shout unto God, living and true,
with the voice of triumph.

Ps. 46 : 3. For the Lord is high, terrible:
a great king over all the earth.
For the most holy Father of heaven,
our king, before ages sent His Beloved Son from on high and He
was born of the Blessed Virgin,
holy Mary.

Ps. 88 : 27. He shall cry out to me: Thou art
my Father ;

Ps. 88 : 28. And I will make Him My First-
born, high above the kings of the
earth.

Ps. 41 : 9. In the day time the Lord hath commanded His mercy : and a canticle
to Him in the night.

Ps. 117 : 24. This is the day which the Lord
hath made : let us rejoice and be
glad in it.
For the beloved and most holy
Child has been given to us and
born for us by the wayside.

Luke 2 : 7. And laid in a manger because He had no room in the inn.

Luke 2 : 14. Glory to God in the highest ; and on earth peace to men of good will.

Ps. 95 : 11. Let the heavens rejoice and the earth be glad, and let the sea be moved and the fulness thereof.

Ps. 95 : 12. The fields shall rejoice and all that are in them.

Ps. 95 : 1. Sing to Him a new canticle ; sing to the Lord, all the earth.

Ps. 95 : 4. For the Lord is great and exceedingly to be praised : He is to be feared above all gods.

Ps. 95 : 7. Bring to the Lord, O ye kindreds of the gentiles, bring to the Lord glory and honor.

Ps. 95 : 8. Bring to the Lord glory unto His Name. Bring your own bodies and bear His holy cross and follow His most holy precepts even unto the end.

And note that this Psalm is said from Christmas until the octave of the Epiphany at all the Hours.

APPENDIX

APPENDIX.

SOME LOST, DOUBTFUL, AND SPURIOUS WRITINGS.

DOUBTLESS we should have expected every fragment of St. Francis' writings to have been preserved with loving care throughout the ages. But when we consider the conditions under which some of them were composed and the vicissitudes they afterwards passed through, we need not be surprised if all of them have not come down to us. On the contrary. For if we may believe such writers as Ubertino da Casale, serious attempts were made in certain quarters toward the close of the thirteenth century to suppress altogether part of the Saint's writings.[1] Be this as it may, it is certain that several of these precious documents disappeared in the course of time. Among such lost treasures we must reckon the primitive Rule of the Friars in the form approved by Innocent III in 1209.[2] Again only two fragments seem to have survived of the "many writings" which, as has been already mentioned, St. Francis addressed to the Poor Ladies at St.

---

[1] "Et toto conatu fuerunt solliciti annulare scripta beati patris nostri Francisci, in quibus sua intentio de observantia regulae declaratur."—See *Archiv.*, III, pp. 168–169.

[2] See above, p. 26.

Damian's.[1]   Whether or not either of these
fragments is to be identified with a letter written by St. Francis to console the Clares, of
which we read in the *Speculum* and the *Conformities*, it is well nigh impossible to determine.[2]   Celano speaks[3] of a letter to St. Antony
of Padua, different apparently from the one
known to us, and of others to Cardinal Ugolino.[4]
So, too, Eccleston[5] tells of letters written to the
brothers in France and at Bologna.[6]

As to the famous letter of St. Francis to St.
Antony commissioning the latter to teach theology, there is no small diversity of opinion.   It
is given for the first time in the *Liber Miraculo-
rum*,[7] and also in the *Chron. XXIV Generalium*.[8]
M. Sabatier, who was, I believe, the first to call
the authenticity of this letter into question,[9]

---

[1] We need not despair of finding others; the Clares'
archives have mostly escaped spoliation.

[2] See *Spec. Perf.* (ed. Sabatier), c. 108, and ed. Lemmens,
c. 18.   See also the *Conformities* (I, fol. 185), and above,
p. 75.

[3] See 2 Cel. 3, 99.

[4] See 1 Cel. 82.   See also *Leg III Soc.*, 67, where the
Incipit of the letters is given.

[5] *De Adventu Minorum in Angliam.*   See *Mon. Germ.
Hist., Script.*, t. XXVIII, p. 563, and *Anal. Franc.*, t. I, p. 232,
note 4.   See also Fr. Cuthbert's translation of Eccleston, p.
64.

[6] Prof. Herkless in his *Francis and Dominic*, p. 54, cites
some passages from a letter which St. Francis "wrote to his
friends at Bologna" in 1228.   One searches in vain for any
trace of such a letter among the early collections of St.
Francis' writings.

[7] See ed. *Acta S.S.*, no. 20.

[8] See *Anal. Franc.*, t. III, p. 132.

[9] *Vie de S. François*, p. 322.

now seems less inclined to reject it.[1] Professor Goetz[2] has decided for, and Professor Boehmer[3] against it. The Quaracchi editors, in excluding this letter from their edition of the *Opuscula*, by no means intended to deny that St. Francis wrote to *fratri Antonio*,[4] but they were unable to determine which if any of the three different forms of this letter now in circulation might be the genuine one. Since the matter is *sub judice*,[5] so to say, I think, with Mr. Carmichael, this letter might find a place among the " Doubtful Works " of St. Francis.[6]

Apropos of the Saint's doubtful works it seems proper to say a word as to the Rule of the Brothers and Sisters of Penance. Although this Rule—like that of the Clares—is wanting in all the early MS. collections of St. Francis' writings, we know from Bernard of Besse[7] that St.

---

[1] See *Opuscules*, fasc. x, p. 128, note 1.

[2] *Die Quellen*, etc., p. 20. He places its composition between 1222 and 1225.

[3] *Analekten*, p. vii.

[4] In the Liegnitz MS. and the Vatican Codex 4354 the present letter is addressed *fratri Antonio episcopo meo*, which corresponds with the direction given by Celano (2 Cel. 3, 99).

[5] On this letter see also Papini (*Storia*, t. I, p. 118, n. 1), Müller (*Anfänge*, p. 103), Lempp (*Zeitschrift*, t. XII, pp. 425, 438), Lepitre (*S. Antoine*, p. 73), and de Kerval (*S. Antonii*, etc., p. 259, n. 1).

[6] Another less well known letter to St. Antony, giving him permission " to build a church near the city wall of Patti," is sometimes attributed to St. Francis. But the text is most improbable and gives rise to colossal historic difficulties. See Lepitre, *S. Antoine*, p. 120, note, and Fr. Edouard d'Alençon, *Etudes Franc.*, t. XII, p. 361.

[7] *Liber de Laudibus* in *Anal. Franc.*, t. III, p. 686.

Francis, with the coöperation of Cardinal Ugolino, wrote a Rule for these Tertiaries. What
became of this document? It is generally
conceded that the Rule of this Third Order as
it stands in the Bull *Supra montem* of Nicholas
IV in 1289[1] is not the handiwork of St. Francis ;
and for the rest the early history of the Third
Order is uncertain, as all Franciscan students are
aware.[2] But what are we to think of the much
older text of this Rule published by M. Sabatier
in 1901, after MS. XX of the convent at Capistran in the Abruzzi?[3] Father Mandonnet, O.P.,
has tried to prove that the first twelve of the
thirteen chapters comprising this document dis-
covered by M. Sabatier, represent the Rule of
1221 in its primitive state.[4] I would fain share
the opinion of the learned Dominican on this
head, but the objection raised against it by the
Quaracchi editors seems to me insuperable. It
amounts to this : In Chapter VI, § 4, of this
Regula Antiqua there is a clear allusion to a

The text of this Rule (which was the one in force for Franciscan Tertiaries until the promulgation of the Apostolic Con-
stitution *Misericors Dei Filius*, by Leo XIII, May 30, 1883)
may be found in *Seraph. Legisl.*, pp. 77–94. For the new Rule
substituted by Leo XIII, see *Acta ad Tertium Franciscalem
Ordinem spectantia* (Quaracchi, 1901), pp. 72–87.

[2] See *Anal. Boll.*, t. xviii, p. 294.

[3] *Regula Antiqua Fratrum et Sororum de Poenitentia*.
See *Opuscules*, t. I, p. 17. Boehmer also gives the text in his
Analekten.

[4] " La règle donnée en 1221 . . . dans son état primitif."
See his Les Règles et le gouvernement de l'ordo de poenitentia
au XIIIe Siècle in *Opuscules*, t. I, p. 175.

Bull of March 30, 1228,[1] which it is difficult to regard as an interpolation. Moreover, as Fr. Ubald d'Alençon points out,[2] the mention of coin in circulation at Ravenna is also hard to explain in an Umbrian writer. Perhaps this document may prove to be St. Francis' Rule for Tertiaries put into legislative form, with the addition of a few minor regulations. Meanwhile, following the example of the Quaracchi editors, I have abstained from including it among the authentic writings of St. Francis.[3]

Coming next to St. Francis' poems, although he doubtless wrote some few canticles besides the Canticle of the Sun, the two others given by Wadding can hardly be accepted as his, at least in their present form. I refer to the *Amor de caritade*[4] and *In foco l'amor mi mise*.[5] True, they are both attributed to St. Francis by St. Bernardine of Siena,[6] but they are also found among the works of Jacopone da Todi,[7] although Ozanam thinks that at most they were only retouched by the latter.[8] The tendency nowadays is to ascribe

---

[1] The Bull *Detestanda humani generis* of Gregory IX.

[2] *Opuscules de S. François*, p. 28.

[3] There is an English translation of it. See *Third Orders*, etc., by Adderley and Marson (Mowbray, 1902).

[4] Rosetti translated part of this poem in his *Dante and his Circle*, attributing it to St. Francis.

[5] See *Misc. Franc.*, 1888, pp. 96 and 190, for two interesting texts of this poem.

[6] *Opera omnia*, t. IV, sermo 16 and 4 (see *Acta S.S.*, t. II, Oct., p. 1003).

[7] Jacopone, lib. VI, chap. XVI, and lib. VII, chap. VI,

[8] *Les Poètes Franciscains*, p. 90.

all the early Franciscan poetry to Jacopone. When the critical edition of this extraordinary man's works is published at Quaracchi, some needed light will no doubt be thrown on this delicate question ; then too, perhaps, Pacifico, the "King of Verses," and "most courtly doctor of singers," may at length come into his own. Meanwhile a number of poems found in a fifteenth century manuscript at the National Library at Naples, once at the convent of Aquila in the Abruzzi, and lately ascribed to St. Francis, are clearly apocryphal, as Professor Ildebrando della Giovanna has sufficiently demonstrated.

Wadding himself regarded the seven sermons of St. Francis he gives as of doubtful authenticity. ·And rightly, for they are from the work of Fr. Louis Rebolledo, already mentioned.[1] The twenty-eight *Collationes* are, *pace* Fr. Mandonnet, who regards them as genuine,[2] rightly rejected by Professor Goetz, who points out how Wadding compiled them from various sources.[3] Many are translated from an Italian MS. at Fano in the Marches of which we know neither the age nor the parentage.[4] But they seem to be mere transcripts from the early legends. Thus *Collatio I* is an adaptation of Celano (1, 2)

[1] See Wadding, *Opusc.*, p. 508 ff.

[2] See his *Les Origines de l'ordo de Poenitentia ;* see also the *Révue Thomiste*, pp. 295–314.

[3] *Quellen*, etc., XXII, 362. But see above, p. 89, n. 1 also.

[4] "Codiculus quidam vestustus MS. Italico idiomati exaratus mihi à Fano Piceni urbe, ad Metaurum amnem extructa, transmissus." See Wadding, *Opusc.*, p. 285.

and *Collatio XIV* is taken almost verbatim from St. Bonaventure, while *Collatio V* is an accommodation of Celano and St. Bonaventure; *XXVI* and *XXVIII* are abridged from the *Speculum ;* *XXIV* is found in the *Chron. XXIV Gen.*, and so on. It is therefore to the authors of these works and not to St. Francis that these conferences are to be ascribed.

At the end of his edition of the *Opuscula* Wadding has collected several "Prayers of St. Francis" of which the text is more than doubtful. Let us see why. Take for example the prayers said to have been used by St. Francis "at the beginning of his conversion" or "in time of sickness" or "at the elevation." One searches in vain among the early MS. collections for any trace of these prayers, nor is mention of them to be found[1] elsewhere. As regards the prayer "to obtain Poverty," it has long been known that it was not written by St. Francis himself. Wadding found it in the *Arbor Vitae* (l. v., cap. iii), but Ubertino da Casale is there quoting from the *Sacrum Commercium B. Francisci cum Domina Paupertate*.[2] The latter work is not an historical narrative, but an exquisite allegory in which St. Francis' own tale of his mystic espousals with the Lady Poverty is most poetically expanded by one of his follow-

[1] The text of the prayer "in time of sickness " is given by Bonav. *Leg. Maj.*, XIV, 2.

[2] Latin text published in 1900 by Fr. Ed. d'Alençon, and English translation by Montgomery Carmichael (*The Lady Poverty*) in 1901.

ers,[1] and consequently Ubertino did not pretend
in citing such a work to give this prayer as the
actual composition of Francis.[2]

In some MS. collections and library catalogues
certain works may be found ascribed to St.
Francis which are obviously spurious. For
example, the *Epistola B. Francisci ad Fr. Bernar-
dum*, found in at least two fifteenth century
codices,[3] is nothing else but the letter of St.
Bonaventure *continens XXV memoralia.*[4]

Sbaralea[5] mentions copies of a book of the
" Sayings " of St. Francis as existing at Assisi
and Ferrara,[6] but a careful search has failed to
reveal any trace of them. He also refers to a
MS. (B. 31) in the Vallicellian Library at Rome
in which "the sayings of St. Francis are found
with the Rule,"[7] but this codex is also missing.
In this library, however, there *is* a codex (B. 82,
fol. 141 r) which contains a " Sermon delivered
by St. Francis at the end of his life."[8] The

¹ See *Chron. XXIV Generalium* in *Anal. Franc.*, t. III,
p. 283.

² It is none the less a pearl of Franciscan literature. See
the beautiful rendering of it which forms the appendix to
Mr. Carmichael's translation of the *Sacrum Commercium*.

³ At Vicenza (Bertol. lib. cod. G. I. 10. 24, fol. 89 r), also the
Capistran MS. XXI, fol. 180 r.

⁴ See Bonav. *Opera omnia*, t. VIII, p. 491.

⁵ *Supplementum*, p. 244.

⁶ *Liber Dictorum* cujus initium *Quid faciet homo* et finis
Oratio semper est praemittenda.

⁷ " *Dicta S. Francisci*, cum regula extant," he says.

⁸ It is entitled : " Praedicatio quaedam quam fecit B. Franciscus Fratribus suis circa finem mortis sui corporis." It
abounds in quotations from SS. Basil, Chrysostom, Augustine,
Isidore, Gregory, and Bernard.

number of patristic citations this work contains is alone sufficient to demonstrate its spuriousness.

The Francisci Collationes cum fratribus, catalogued among the Latin MSS. of the Royal Library at Munich [1] as being contained in a fifteenth century MS. at that library (cod. 11354), are a selection from the *Dicta* of the Blessed Brother Giles, as is evident from the *Incipit* of the prologue and the text of the first collation.[2] Their attribution to St. Francis is therefore an error of the catalogue. The *Verba S. Francisci de Paupertate,* mentioned in the same catalogue as contained in Cod. 5998, fol. 189, are an excerpt from Chap. VI of the Second Rule of the Friars Minor.[3]

This attribution of writings to St. Francis which clearly do not belong to him is rarely intentional; it is often the result of error. For the rest, it was easiest for compilers and librarians unacquainted with the authorship of certain Franciscan works, and not eager to undertake deep researches as to their origin, to ascribe them to the common father of all Franciscan literature and the source of its inspiration.

Since every new revelation of St. Francis must be a priceless gain, it is devoutly to be wished that the present energetic research work among

[1] See *Catal. codicum latinorum,* t. II, P. II, p. 17, n. 214.
[2] See *Dicta B. Ægidii* (Quaracchi, 1905), pp. 1-51.
[3] As to the "Perfectiones S. Francisci, quas dedit fratri Junipero," found at Paris (nat. lib., cod. 18327, fol. 158 r), see *Monumenta,* tr. II, fol. 281 r.

the sources of Franciscan history may happily bring to light some of St. Francis' writings not known to us save through the formal attestation of the early legends and chronicles, or at least put us in possession of complete copies of such as have come down to us only in fragmentary form.

Meanwhile I conclude this volume by wishing its readers their full share in the blessing which St. Francis himself has promised to those who receive his words kindly : *Omnes illi et illae, qui ea benigne recipient, benedicat eis Pater et Filius et Spiritus Sanctus. Amen.*

BIBLIOGRAPHY.

THE following list of works is intentionally limited. Its aim is to give collectively and in alphabetical order a fuller reference to the principal and most accessible sources of information cited in the course of the present volume.

Acta Sanctorum quotquot toto orbe coluntur, collegit Joannes Bollandus, etc. (ed. 3).

Actus B. Francisci et Sociorum ejus. Ed. Sabatier, Paris, 1902.

Prof. Alessandri: *Inventario dei Manoscritti della biblioteca del conv. di S. Francesco di Assisi.* Forli, 1894.

Analecta Bollandiana.[1] Brussels.

Analecta Franciscana. Quaracchi.

Matthew Arnold: *Essays in Criticism.* Macmillan, 1875.

Reginald Balfour: *The Seraphic Keepsake.* Burns & Oates, 1905.

Fr. Francisci Bartholi, O.F.M. : *Tractatus de Indulgentia S. Mariae de Portiuncula.* Ed. Sabatier, Paris, 1900.

Fr. Bartholomaeus Pisanus, O.F.M. : *De Conformitate Vitae B. Francisci ad vitam D. N. Jesu Christi.* Milan, 1510.[2]

---

[1] The space devoted by Fr. Van Ortroy, S.J., to Franciscan history in this periodical assumes larger proportions each year.

[2] A critical edition of this work will form Vol. IV of the *Anal. Franc.*

Fr. Bernardus de Bessa, O.F.M.: *Liber de Laudibus B. Francisci.* In *Anal. Franc.*, t. III.

Fr. Bernardo da Fivizzano, O.M.Cap.: *Oposcoli di S. Francesco.* Florence, 1880.

Bibliotheca Hagiographica Latina antiquae et mediae aetatis. Ed. Socii Bollandiani. Brussels.

Prof. H. Boehmer: *Analekten zur Geschichte des Franciscus von Assisi.* Tübingen and Leipzig (Mohr), 1904.

Bullettino Critico di Cose Francescane. Florence.

S. Bonaventura: *Legendae duae de Vita S. Francisci.* Quaracchi, 1898. (English translation by Miss Lockhart. Washbourne, 1898.)

Bullarium Franciscanum. Ed. F. F. Hyacinth Sbaralea and Conrad Eubel, O.M.Conv. 1759 and 1898.

Montgomery Carmichael: *La Benedizione di San Francesco.* Livorno, 1900. "The Origin of the Rule of St. Francis," in *Dublin Review,* Vol. CXXXIV, 1904, pp. 357–385. "The Writings of St. Francis," in the *Month,* January, 1904, t. CIII, pp. 156–164. See also under *Sacrum Commercium.*

Fr. Thomas de Celano, O.F.M.: *Vita Prima S. Francisci.* Ed. Suyskens, S.J., in *Acta S.S.,* Oct., II.

Vita Secunda S. Francisci. Ed. Amoni. Rome, 1880.

Tractatus de Miraculis. Ed. Van Ortroy, S.J., in *Anal. Boll.,* t. XVIII, 1899.

Vita S. Clarae. Ed. Sedulius, O.F.M. Antwerp, 1613.

Fr. Leopold de Chérancé : *S. François d'Assise.* Paris, 1892. (English translation by R. F. O'Connor : Burns & Oates, 1901.)

Fr. Bernard Christen, O.M.Cap. : *Leben des hl. Franciscus von Assisi.* Innsbruck, 1899.

Chronica XXIV Generalium in *Anal. Francis.*, t. III.

Fr. Cuthbert, O.S.F.C. See under Eccleston.

G. Cozza-Luzi : *Chiara di Assisi ed Innocenzo IV.* Rome, 1887.

Lina Duff Gordon : *The Story of Assisi.* Dent, 1901.

Fr. Thomas Eccleston, O.F.M. : *De Adventu Fratrum Minorum in Angliam* in *Anal. Franc.*, t. I ; see *Monumenta Franc.* Ed. Brewer. Rolls series. (English translation by Fr. Cuthbert, O.S.F.C. : *The Friars and how they came to England.* Sands, 1903.)

Fr. Edouard d'Alençon, O.M.Cap. :[1] *Epistola S. Francisci ad Ministrum Generalem in sua forma authentica.* Rome, 1899. *La Benediction de S. François.* Paris, 1896. See also *Sacrum Commercium.*

Fr. Ehrle, S.J. : "Die Historischen Handschriften von S. Francesco in Assisi" in the *Archiv für*

---

[1] When this volume is almost through the press, I learn of the publication of Fr. Edouard's long-promised edition of Celano's works—*S. Francisci Assisiensis vita et miracula additis opusculis liturgicis auctore Fr. Thoma de Celano. Hanc editionem novam ad fidem mss. recensuit P. Eduardus Alenconiensis*, Rome. Desclée, 1905.

Litteratur und Kirchengeschichte des Mittelalters, t. I, pp. 484 seq. "Controversen über die Anfänge des Minoritenordens" in *Zeitschrift für Katholische Theologie*, t. XI, pp. 725 seq.

Mgr. Faloci-Pulignani: "Tre Autografi di S. Francesco" in *Misc. Francescana*, t. VI, pp. 33 seq., and "La Calligrafia di S. Francesco," *l. c.*, t. VII, pp. 67 seq.

Floretum S. Francisci Assisiensis. Ed. Sabatier. Paris, 1902. A satisfactory Italian version of the *Fioretti* is that of Barbere, Florence, 1902. An excellent English translation, *The Little Flowers of St. Francis*, is published by Kegan Paul, 1905.

Etudes Franciscaines. Namur.

Joseph Görres: *Der hl. Franciscus von Assisi, ein Troubadour.* Ratisbon, 1879.

Prof. Walter Goetz: *Die Quellen zur Geschichte des hl. Franz von Assisi.* Gotha, 1904.

Prof. John Herkless: *Francis and Dominic and the Mendicant Orders.* Scribner, 1901.

Fr. Jordani a Jano, O.F.M.: *Chronica*, in *Anal. Franc.*, t. I.

Leon de Kerval: *Sancti Antonii de Padua Vitae duae.* Paris, 1904.

Fr. Leonard Lemmens, O.F.M.: "Die Anfänge des Clarissenordens" in *Römische Quartalschrift*, t. XVI, pp. 93 seq. *Scripta Fratris Leonis*, Quaracchi, 1901. See also under *Speculum Perfectionis*.

Abbé Leon Le Monnier: *Histoire de S. Fran-*

çois d'Assise. (English translation by a Franciscan Tertiary. Kegan Paul, 1894.)

Prof. A. G. Little: *Description de MS. Can. Misc.* 525, de la Bibliothèque Bodleienne. Paris, 1903.

Canon Knox Little: *St. Francis of Assisi: His Times, Life, and Work.* Isbister, 1904.

Anne Macdonnell: *The Words of St. Francis.* Dent, 1905.

Fr. P. Mandonnet, O.P.: *Les Origines de l'Ordo de Poenitentia* (Freiburg, 1898). *Les Regles et le Gouvernement de l'Ordo de Poenitentia au XIIIe Siècle* (Paris, 1902).

Miscellanea Francescana di Storia di Lettere, di Arti. Foligno.

Monumenta Germaniae Historica. Berlin.

Prof. Karl Müller: *Anfänge des Minoritenordens und der Bussbruderschaften.* Freiburg, 1885.

A. F. Ozanam: *Les Poètes Franciscains en Italie au Treizième Siècle.* Paris, 1882, 6th ed.

Opuscula S. P. Francisci Assisiensis. Edita a PP. Collegii S. Bonaventurae, Quaracchi, 1904.

Fr. Panfilo da Magliano, O.F.M.: *Storia Compendiosa di San Francesco.* Rome, 1874–1876.

Paul Sabatier: *Vie de S. François d'Assise.* Paris, 1894. (English translation by L. S. Houghton.) *Regula antiqua Fratrum et Sororum de Poenitentia.* Paris. (English translation in Adderley and Marsons' *Third Orders.* Mowbray, 1902.) *Description du MS. Franciscain de Liegnitz.* Paris, 1901. *Examen de quelques*

Travaux recents sur les Opuscules de Saint François. Paris, 1904. See also under *Actus*, Bartholi, and *Speculum*.

Fr. Hyacinth. Sbaralea, O.M.Conv.: *Supplementum et Castigatio ad Scriptores Trium Ordinum S. Francisci.* Rome, 1806.

Sacrum Commercium Beati Francisci cum Domina Paupertate. Ed. Fr. Ed. d'Alençon, O.M.Cap. Rome, 1900. (English translation by Montgomery Carmichael, *The Lady Poverty;* Murray, 1901.)

Emma Gurney Salter : *Franciscan Legends in Italian Art.* Dent, 1905.

Scraphicae Legislationis Textus Originales. Quaracchi, 1897.

Speculum Perfectionis. Ed. Lemmens: Quaracchi, 1901.

Speculum Perfectionis. Ed. Sabatier. Paris, 1898. (English translation of the text only, by the Countess de la Warr : *The Mirror of Perfection.* Burns & Oates, 1902.)

Luigi Suttina: *Appunti Bibliografici di Studi Francescani.* Padua, 1904.

H. Thode : *Franz von Assisi und die Anfänge der Kunst der Renaissance in Italien.* Berlin, 1885 and 1904.

Trium Sociorum, Legenda S. Francisci Assis. Ed. Faloci. Foligno, 1898. (English translation by E. Gurney Salter: *The Legend of the Three Companions.* Dent, 1902.)

Fr. Ubald d'Alençon, O.M.Cap. : *Les Opuscules de S. François d'Assise.* Paris, 1905.

Fr. Van Ortroy, S.J. For his article on the *Opuscula* of St. Francis, see *Analecta Bollandiana*, t. xxiv, fasc. iii (1905), p. 411 seq.

Fr. Luke Wadding, O.F.M.: *Annales Minorum.*[1] *B. P. Francisci Assisiatis Opuscula.* Antwerp, 1623. *Scriptores Ordinis Minorum.* Rome, 1650.

[1] Wadding's *Annales* appeared at Lyons in 8 vols. in fol. 1625–54. Fr. Jos. Man. Fonseca published a new edition and a continuation of the *Annales* in 19 vols. at Rome, 1731–45. The official Annalists of the Friars Minor have since added 6 vols. (tom. 20–25), which were issued at Naples, Ancona, and Quaracchi. The last vol. (t. 25) edited by Fr. Eusebius Fernandzin († 1899) extends to the year 1622. The Quaracchi Friars are now engaged on the 26th volume.

INDEX.

Made in the USA
Monee, IL
12 April 2024

56822096R10134